Leadership
From Inside Out

Books by the Author

Worldly Spirituality
Ecology and Life
Tending the Garden
Redeeming the Creation

Leadership
From Inside Out

Spirituality and
Organizational Change

Wesley Granberg-Michaelson

Foreword by Jim Wallis

A Crossroad Book
The Crossroad Publishing Company
New York

The Crossroad Publishing Company
www.crossroadpublishing.com

The text is set in 12/15 Goudy Old Style. The display types are Scala and Kabel.

Printed in the United States of America

Library of Congress Cataloging-in-Publication Data
Granberg-Michaelson, Wesley.
    Leadership from inside out : spirituality and organizational change / Wesley Granberg-Michaelson ; foreword by Jim Wallis.
        p.   cm.
    Includes bibliographical references and index.
    ISBN 0-8245-2137-4 (alk. paper)
    1. Leadership – Religious aspects – Christianity.   I. Title.
BV4597.53.L43G73 2004
658.4′092– dc22
                                                                    2004014959

To Gordon Cosby,
mentor, pastor, and model of a leader

Contents

About Leadership

Jim Wallis

The alternative to bad leadership must not become *no* leadership; it should rather be good leadership. As obvious as that point should be, the massive and very public failures of so many leaders, who have misused or abused their authority in almost every sector of our society — political, business, civil, and even religious — have helped create a powerful anti-leadership culture. The popular bumper sticker "Question Authority" says it all and captures the cultural antagonism toward leadership. But without leadership — good leadership — we are in serious trouble. Leadership can appeal to our best or worst values and instincts, take us backward or move us forward, further divide us or bring us together to accomplish important things. But without leadership we are unlikely to act together to fulfill our best impulses and values.

There are three reasons why you should read this book. First, it is one of the clearest summaries you're likely to find anywhere of the best books and ideas about leadership available today. Second, it takes that *knowledge* a significant step deeper into *wisdom;* this is not just about the skills of leadership, but the spirituality of leadership. Third, it is written by an actual leader, not just somebody with thoughts about leadership.

I have known Wes Granberg-Michaelson for more than three decades and have watched him lead — in the political, non-profit, and religious arenas. And quite frankly, I have never seen a better leader in action. Whether it is leading a meeting or an organization, drawing diverse people together or helping them clarify a unified message, resolving conflicts or offering a prophetic word when one is necessary — Wes is one of the best I've ever known. Read this book, and learn how to be an effective leader, but also one who has moral and spiritual integrity.

Wes starts by dealing with the central problem of a leader's need to control, and focuses on the three classic areas of money, sex, and power. Then he focuses in particular on the need for a new ethic in regard to economics, obviously critical in today's climate of financial corruption. While acknowledging the crucial corrective of mistrusting leadership, he explores the deeper social quest for a genuinely trustworthy leadership. Accepting our vulnerabilities rather than denying them is central to good leadership; as is the critical formation of character as a lifelong pursuit.

Leaders must learn how to identify values, build integrity, and sustain vision, says Granberg-Michaelson. Listening for one's *calling* is essential for good leadership, as is a self-definition that is not just about the work. Freedom from inner needs requires a spiritual self-awareness that can save us (and others around us) from our unresolved issues. Don't try to be a well-rounded leader, says the author, but rather know your own gifts and strengths well enough to match them with what your co-workers can bring. In the end, it is better to understand yourself than to force the others around you to keep trying to figure you out! And self-knowledge requires a spiritual journey.

Wes is especially good at changing organizational cultures, instilling new values, and getting people to decide how they will decide things; and he shows you how to do that too. But he doesn't just focus on the "techniques" of effective leadership but on how to see the "big picture" and "cast the vision." The author reminds us that "change is messy," but for it to happen well we need to focus on the three critical elements of time, participation, and trust. Creating a "road map" is absolutely key if vision is ever to issue forth in any real new direction. "Vision without strategy is like faith without works," says Granberg-Michaelson, which is a word I would like most leaders I know to hear very deeply. There is no best leadership style, as some would suggest, but different styles of leadership that are called for in different situations, at different stages in an organization's life, or even different periods of a leader's life.

The challenge of organizational growth is enormous, and even more so is what the author calls the "arduous journey of transformation" for leaders. "Charisma alone in a leader is not enough, for inspiring people is not the same as leading them," says Wes Granberg-Michaelson. I'll say an "Amen" to that. I've discovered that the experience of leadership feels just as Wes describes, like "driving by faith." And this book is full of good driving lessons for leaders.

1

What Leaders Need to Control

Most leaders focus on how to succeed in a task. A far better approach is to focus on who you are. It is said that the unexamined life is not worth living. Certainly, the unexamined life is unequipped for leading, and the cost of leaders who act blindly or in denial of their own weaknesses is devastating. People suffer needlessly. Trust is betrayed. Entire organizations can be crippled.

Three human needs have the capacity to destroy any leader: money, sex, and power. It is no wonder that even early monastic communities established three vows for those called to religious leadership: poverty, chastity, and obedience. These vows were, of course, severe protective measures to guard against the potentially fatal compulsion of these three needs. But they did underscore the crucial importance of controlling those needs that otherwise can totally control us — money, sex, and power. Individuals whose lives are controlled by the unbridled quest for any one of these eventually will find their effectiveness as leaders put in jeopardy and may be likely as well to damage the institution they were called to serve. Of course, the monastic solutions of the Middle Ages are still faithfully followed by hundreds of thousands of people committed in religious orders today, but when even a few break these vows and others attempt to shield them from accountability, faith in the integrity of religious institutions is shattered.

Obviously, vows of poverty, chastity, and obedience are not the only safeguards for dealing with the temptations of money, sex, and power in our lives. Since the Reformation of Martin Luther and John Calvin in the sixteenth century, the church has stressed faithful stewardship, covenantal love, and self-giving service as healthy responses to these human realities, with the emphasis placed on controlling, directing, and redeeming the needs for money, sex, and power rather than denying them.

The Reformation tradition stressed that money, sex, and power are not evil in and of themselves but a part of God's good creation, so that what matters instead is how they are used. Individuals — rather than political or religious hierarchies — came to assume more responsibility for determining in practice how to respond to these needs. Of course, objective moral guidelines remained, especially regarding sex but even in this area, the affirmation was that sexuality, within the covenant of marriage, was good and to be enjoyed, rather than simply serving the purpose of procreation, and thereby created new expectations for how individuals would use this gift.

Over time, the church's attitude toward money, sex, and power shifted as the role of each within society was changing radically, and we can leave to others the debate about whether the church changed society or society changed the church. But one simply needs to compare how sin was characterized in the Middle Ages to subsequent notions of sin that evolved over the last couple of centuries to see the difference. Much of this change reflects a deeper understanding of both biblical truth and the human situation, and I dare-say that few people today would want to conduct their lives within the economic, social, religious, and political norms of the Middle Ages.

Three human needs have the capacity to destroy any leader: money, sex, and power.

For example, take the concept of "prelacy." It refers to the pride of place or position, and it used to be widely regarded as a moral danger and real temptation. Today most of us would have difficulty even defining the word. Further, we take it for granted that attaining a higher "position," whether in business, politics, or the church, is an accomplishment that should make us feel good about ourselves. Whether we say so or not, most of us take pride in our accomplishments and gain psychic currency from any important position we achieve.

Even more pointedly, consider the sin of avarice. "An inordinate desire of gaining and possessing wealth," says the Webster's dictionary, that is to say, a synonym for covetousness. In the theology of the Middle Ages, avarice was one of the "seven deadly sins," meaning it was so grave a danger that spiritual death could result, but the engine of the modern globalized economy runs on the fuel of avarice and covetousness. Every day we are being persuaded, through hundreds of messages, to "covet" and buy something others have.

More simply, think for a moment of the sin of gluttony — eating too much. It, too, was one of the Middle Ages' seven deadly sins, meaning, it can put our souls in peril. And yet today, with Zagat restaurant guides downloaded onto our Palm Pilots, this attitude seems almost ludicrous. Indeed, refined feasting has become a fine art, but in the mind-set of the Middle Ages, the hoarding of possessions — and the fruit of the land was one of the most basic commodities — was considered so serious a character flaw that it endangered one's soul.

The modern era has instead sought to make its peace with money, sex, and power. It's true that these three needs are all parts of God's good creation, and without them, life itself would be impossible. But it seems as if we live nowadays as though we are immune to the dangers — yes, even the mortal dangers — that these three human needs, when not controlled, can pose to our souls. Of course they have potential for good. We know all the vocabulary about the responsible use of power, and responsible sex, and being responsible as good stewards, all to create what one ethicist has called "the responsible society." But let us not be naïve about the dangers they pose to us. Money, sex, and power have a subtle but persistent ability, especially in contemporary society, to cloud our judgment, to corrode our values, and to capture our will, in the end, leading us to behave in ways that are flagrantly irresponsible.

Society seems so disillusioned with so much of its leadership today in politics, business, and religion, and yet people yearn deeply for leaders, and especially, one hears again and again, leaders whom they can trust. *Let me suggest where this search for trustworthy leaders might start: beneath all the other necessary qualities in a leader, we should look for individuals who have demonstrated the inner capacity to deal creatively and responsibly with money, sex, and power in their lives.* Directing the energy of these three human needs into stewardship, covenantal love, and service is finally a spiritual task. For centuries men and women have followed paths and practices that transform these three needs into joyous gifts rather than destructive compulsions. Leaders who can be trusted to guide the evolution of institutions into the future will be those who lead well-examined lives, who have recovered spiritual practices that liberate them from the power of compulsions and free their energy for outward service.

2

In the Service of Mammon

Money is the idol operative in most of our lives, controlling many of the decisions we make, permeating our values, and motivating many of our actions. Achieving freedom from the dominating power of money in our lives requires hard work in our souls.

Part of the process of liberating ourselves from the idolatry of money involves distinguishing between our economic needs and our desires, weighing which desires seem justifiable and economically possible, and which are in fact excessive and wasteful. Even more difficult perhaps, is determining an ethical framework for making economic choices when living in a society of abundance and a world of scarcity.

Such dilemmas concerning money face us all, rich and poor alike. Trappist monks, living under a vow of poverty and sharing their possessions in community, wonder if they are justified in owning their expanse of land in order to protect their solitude. None of us ever really escapes the need to ask economic questions of our lives and make daily choices about money. The basic test we all face, it seems, is whether we have control over the power of money or whether the power of money controls us.

Ironically, acquiring more money doesn't necessarily free us from its forceful grip on our lives, and instead more money enslaves us more. When we are held captive to material gain, we risk losing our souls — meaning, our center of ethical coherence, moral direction, and spiritual identity. As Jesus said, "You cannot serve God and wealth" (Matt. 6:24). The teachings of Jesus regarding money are emphatic, radical, and difficult to follow faithfully. Mary's Magnificat, anticipating the birth of Jesus, promises that "the rich will be sent away empty." Jesus asks the rich young ruler to sell his possessions if he is to follow; he can't. The difficulties of the rich being part of the kingdom of God are described in metaphors like a camel getting through the eye of a needle and in stories like the rich man who builds larger barns for his possessions, but who is called a fool by God and condemned (Luke 12:13–21).

This tension concerning money has particular relevance for leaders. Often — although not always — our leaders are rewarded more generously than others for their greater responsibilities. From the viewpoint of the institution, such compensation expresses the value the leaders have in the eyes of the organizations they serve. But for the leaders, the monetary compensation can sharpen the question of inner motivation: How important is monetary reward to my service?

Recently I heard a sportscaster describe a fine baseball player who had chosen to stay with his team and turned down an offer of significantly more money, out of loyalty to the organization and enjoyment of his teammates. Of course he was already making a very comfortable salary, but what struck me was how unusual this situation was. Most players, when they become free agents and have the chance, migrate to the highest bidder, and even with salaries in the millions, other values don't usually override the amount of cold cash on the table. If given the chance, would any of us act differently?

The teachings of Jesus regarding money are emphatic, radical, and difficult to follow faithfully.

If in the end we are in servitude to wealth, we also run the danger of blurring choices involving our ethical integrity. High-profile scandals in the business world during the past few years have demonstrated the destructive potential of sacrificing integrity, individually or collectively, for economic gain. Enron, one of the country's largest corporations, lost virtually all of its massive economic value because its accounting practices were ethically compromised by several key leaders so driven by corporate and personal greed that they lost all ability to make simple moral judgments about right and wrong. While the corporation's leadership fought criminal charges, its employees lost both their savings and livelihood.

Martha Stewart, America's house and garden mentor, apparently couldn't resist, according to charges, acting unethically on insider trader information to protect just a small portion of her fortune. Former U.S. Senator Robert Toricelli from New Jersey withdrew from his bid for reelection in 2002 only a month before the vote because of persistent allegations that he improperly received gifts and granted favors in exchange.

Examples of business executives and public figures who become corrupted by the power of money and greed have proliferated in recent years. But more troubling, and harder to face, are instances when religious leaders compromise their financial integrity. Consider, for example, the painful case of Rev. Allan Boesak. An outstanding theologian and anti-apartheid leader in South Africa, Boesak displayed rare leadership skills. In a critical period, Boesak was elected president of the World Alliance of Reformed Churches, which dramatically broke fellowship and communion with the white South African Reformed Church persisting in its defense of apartheid.

Within South Africa Allan Boesak was regarded as a key religious leader in the struggle against apartheid. Throughout the world church his reputation grew. Many thought of him as potential leader in any post-apartheid South Africa. I well remember a small dinner meeting with him after he was elected president of the World Alliance of Reformed Churches. Boesak was bright, witty, theologically sharp, politically adroit, and entertaining. One could sense his leadership ability, and it was common for others to speculate about what high office Boesak would come to hold in a new South Africa.

But then problems began to appear in the funds of his Foundation for Peace and Justice. An article in the *Christian Century*, "What Happened to Allan Boesak?" by Sarah Ruden (June 21–28, 2000, pp. 670–71) provided one appraisal of this sad story and its aftermath. The financial accounts of the foundation, which had received funding from many European church agencies, were in disarray. Boesak and his second wife (whom he married after his first marriage ended with charges of his adultery) were known for their posh lifestyle, spending thousands conspicuously with no other apparent source of money than his foundation. "So heartless were the thefts that a member of Boesak's own organization finally blew the whistle," writes Ruden, at which point the church agencies in Europe had no choice but to cut off funding, a move Boesak's supporters saw as foreign self-righteousness. I recall well when a close friend of mine and key supporter of Boesak's foundation from one of the Scandinavian church agencies told me of his utter disappointment and dismay over what was discovered. What disturbed my friend the most was how a person with such unique gifts and potential as Boesak could so carelessly and mortally damage himself.

The case eventually went to court. Boesak refused to testify in his own defense and claimed that his foundation was a front for the African National Congress. But according to Ruden, "Undisputed documents and impeccable witnesses leave little doubt about Boesak's guilt." After a lengthy appeal process, a guilty verdict was upheld and he was sentenced to jail.

Many still wonder what happened to erode Allan Boesak's moral compass. One can only assume that what began for him as small ethical rationalizations about using foundation donations for personal purposes, so easy to make when struggling for a just cause, began to grow and become habitual, until it became his way of life. Indeed, financial enrichment has a subtle capacity to undermine ethical discernment even in gifted leaders committed to social justice and human welfare, and the rightness of the goals leaders seek in their work can never excuse them from the demands of acting with personal moral integrity.

Jesus was realistic and right about the captivating power money can have in our lives. Within an intensely materialistic society, deep spiritual discipline is required to maintain freedom from the idolatry of wealth and its potentially destructive consequences. Jesus' instructions to his followers about the role of money in our lives are clear: "Do not keep striving for what you are to eat and what you are to drink, and do not keep worrying. . . . Sell your possessions, and give alms. . . . For where your treasure is, there your heart will be also" (Luke 12:29, 33a, 34). Any who wish to be free enough to lead effectively need to ask — and to keep asking — whether they are truly serving God or the idol of wealth.

3

Blind Mistrust

President Richard Nixon began his second term in 1973 after a landslide victory over George McGovern, carrying every state but Massachusetts. Continuing to forge a dramatically new international political landscape, he opened diplomatic and economic doors to China and put a strategic arms limitation treaty into place with the Soviets. Nixon's sweeping reelection, according to political observers, likewise gave him a mandate for carrying out ambitious domestic initiatives as well, but by August 1974, less than two years later he became the first U.S. president to resign from office.

Why? No left-wing vendetta brought Nixon down, nor did a conspiracy of opponents in the press. Flaws in Richard Nixon's own character were what led ultimately to his undoing, for he had never learned how to deal gracefully with power. As the famous White House tapes gave the nation a picture of his inner life, we came to see what governed so much of Nixon's political and personal actions. It appears that he never really felt safe. He was paranoid toward those whom he suspected were his enemies. He seemed incapable of sustained trust, driven by a zealous need for self-protection, and dominated by a vengeful desire to attack those who opposed him. More than the typical rough and tumble tactics of political life, for President Nixon, a deep inward insecurity impelled him to fight, control, and manipulate everyone possible in a quest for political security.

Lest the reader dismiss these reflections as mere conjecture, I should say that they are based on my own personal observation and experience. At the time I was working as an assistant to U.S. Senator Mark O. Hatfield. A lifelong Republican, Hatfield had supported Nixon's nomination for president in 1968 and was nearly selected as his vice presidential running mate. But Hatfield had also steadfastly opposed U.S. intervention in Vietnam, and, with George McGovern, led an attempt in the U.S. Senate to stop funding for the war.

Mark Hatfield was a politician guided by strong moral principles. As a deeply committed Christian, he sought to integrate his understanding of faith with the decisions and demands of public service, and so was regarded by nearly all as a gracious and compassionate public figure, without any true enemies in the U.S. Senate, even among those with whom he had sharp disagreements. Whenever there was an illness or tragedy in the family of a fellow senator, Hatfield responded personally with calls, caring words, and prayers. He knew those who served in the Senate dining room by name, always asking about their families. In politics he always understood that today's opponent may need to be tomorrow's ally, and so he worked hard to build relationships and keep doors open, making sure that political adversaries would not become personal enemies.

And yet for all the goodwill he had, Hatfield eventually learned that he had one very powerful enemy who lived at 1600 Pennsylvania Avenue — President Richard Nixon. As it later came to light, Nixon had compiled a list of those

whom he regarded as absolute foes and instructed key staff
to use powers taking measures against them, as enemies. In
opposing Nixon's Vietnam policies, Hatfield had earned a
place on this "enemies" list, and his shaky relationship with
the president steadily deteriorated.

Moreover, Nixon's enmity toward Hatfield didn't stop
there. We learned that, as Hatfield's chief staff person dealing with Vietnam and other policy issues, I had been placed
under secret government surveillance. I had traveled to
South Vietnam and Cambodia at that time, talking both
with embassy officials and opponents of U.S. policy, and,
with another staff colleague, I met the North Vietnamese
representatives in Paris at the peace talks to discuss U.S.
prisoners of war and related issues. Though in these matters
I was carrying out my role as a staff assistant to a U.S. senator,
given the climate of the Nixon administration, government
intelligence agencies covertly followed and monitored my
activities. Others active in the antiwar movement were sub-
jected to the same tactics, including former government
officials who had resigned in protest over Nixon's Vietnam
policies. In my case, years later I requested my "files" through
the government's Freedom of Information Act. When they
finally came, much of the text of the documents I received
was blacked out "for security reasons." But the pattern of
secret surveillance was revealed clearly.

These days tested the integrity of my own Christian faith.
I was raised in a conservative evangelical environment, and
most of my relatives and Christian friends were strongly supportive of Nixon and his Vietnam policies. But because of
my Christian convictions, I had come to strongly oppose our
actions in Vietnam, and much else in our nation's military
policies. It bred a personal isolation from many others, yet

formed a strong bond with Hatfield, whose personal experience was so similar to my own. Meeting people like Jim
Wallis, who had begun a magazine called the *Post-American*
and held similar evangelical and antiwar convictions, as well
as theologians like the late John Howard Yoder, who wrote
The Politics of Jesus, helped undergird my antiwar activism
with foundational Christian convictions. That was essential
in this time of bitter political divisions and public religious
confusion on such central moral challenges.

**Even if this attitude of distrust has been a healthy
corrective over time, our contemporary quest for
credible and trustworthy leadership in our society's
institutions has its roots in the disillusionment created
by the actions of a paranoid president finally forced
to resign from office.**

My own experience of being under government surveillance reflected the larger web of suspicion, mistrust, and
retaliation with its roots finally in the insecurity of Richard
Nixon, the measure of which became clear in the Watergate scandal. Despite his political dominance over George
McGovern and a deeply divided Democratic Party heading
into the 1972 election, Nixon and his aides authorized various illegal activities to gain political information, including a
break-in at the Watergate offices of the Democratic National
Committee. As the White House's role in this criminal activ-
ity began to be revealed, Nixon responded by authorizing a
cover-up. As is so often the case, the most damaging actions
of this leader were not the original transgressions, which

could have been acknowledged and politically defused by forceful actions to dismiss those responsible. Instead, Nixon's inability to admit any error and his action in obstructing the process of public accountability became politically fatal.

In the end, Richard Nixon's insecurity undermined the trust of a whole citizenry in their government, with the result that my generation — I was in my twenties at the time — developed an automatic suspicion of the government's power and of economic and educational institutions. Even if this attitude of distrust has been a healthy corrective over time, our contemporary quest for credible and trustworthy leadership in our society's institutions has its roots in the disillusionment created by the actions of a paranoid president finally forced to resign from office.

Nixon's weaknesses were human, and like our own they were also correctable, redeemable. He could have discovered how to control his acute suspicions of those not always loyal to him. Nixon could have been helped to check his tendency to punish those whom he believed were his enemies. He could have learned how to resist a desire for revenge. But he didn't.

Many writers, historians, and political analysts have tried to understand the psychological make-up of this complex leader. The picture that emerges is of a man oblivious to his own weaknesses and clearly unable to be vulnerable with others who wished to be nurturing and supportive. Most revealing were the comments of Billy Graham, a long friend of Nixon (and Mark Hatfield). When the Watergate tapes were released, Graham was amazed, for they portrayed a person whom Graham felt he had not known.

So in the end, Richard Nixon's inability to understand his own weaknesses cost him his presidency. The chain of events, from the creation of lists of enemies, to the "plumbers," to dirty tricks, to hush money, to denials and the obstruction of justice, can all be traced to dangerous, unchecked traits in Nixon's personality, in particular his insecurity. His desire to cling to power as a way to deal with his insecurity ultimately left him blind to his own vulnerabilities and thus unable to control himself. In the words of the Proverb, "It is better to win control over yourself than over whole cities" (Prov. 16:32).

4

A Denial of Vulnerability

Twenty-five years after Richard Nixon's resignation, un-controlled sex rather than unchecked power devastated the nation's trust in another president, Bill Clinton, in yet another example of an extraordinarily gifted leader nearly destroyed by denying his own vulnerability. With Clinton, the specific weakness involved his handling of his sexual drives rather than managing insecurity through vindictive actions to maintain power, but the larger point is the same: the inner life of a leader, in the end, directly affects whether he or she is able to truly lead.

In late January 1999, when the allegations of Bill Clinton's sexual relationship with Monica Lewinsky had just recently become public, Clinton faced the daunting task of addressing the National Prayer Breakfast. This annual event gathers members of Congress, the cabinet, and hundreds of other leaders from various sectors of society for a morning to acknowledge a shared spiritual dependence upon God. A few of Clinton's friends urged him to simply make a humble, even if general, confession of wrong, ask for forgiveness, and promise to recommit himself to his responsibilities of leadership. In retrospect, such a gesture, at that point, might well have ended this whole episode as a matter of national obsession. However, Clinton listened not only to his pastoral friends, but also to his political pollster, Dick Morris, and Morris told him that because Clinton had initially denied any wrongdoing, the perception of perjury — not just adultery — would be politically costly. In other words, a simple confession wasn't polling well; so Clinton decided he had to deny any wrongdoing, try to cover up, and fight.

Most of us know the saga that unfolded in the following months. By August 1999, before a group of pastors in the White House, Clinton finally offered an honest confession, knowing by then that DNA testing of a stained dress proved beyond any doubt that he had been a persuasive, artful liar. I remember listening on the radio to his talk before that group of pastors, a heartfelt and personalized recounting of Psalm 51, linked to his own failings. Unfortunately, it had come nine months too late, a confession not freely offered but forced by the evidence. The political damage already had been done, to both his presidency and to the nation's already frail trust in its leaders.

Like Nixon, Bill Clinton had a weakness, familiar to many who knew him, a flaw that was correctable, redeemable. Instead of self-control he chose the path of public denial, such that his well-rehearsed, finger-pointing declaration of no sex with "that woman" became a televised icon open to public ridicule. It was his self-righteous deceptiveness even to his best friends rather than the sexual transgressions per se that so eroded our trust in Bill Clinton's character and leadership.

Leadership today requires people of character who are capable of creating a climate of trust, identifying values, building integrity, and sustaining vision. After Nixon and

Clinton, the character of leaders counts more than even before, for it is not enough that leaders simply have the right skills. People yearn for leadership that is morally seamless, not in a futile quest for leaders whom we expect to be perfect, but in a legitimate expectation that we be led by individuals who seek to embed their lives in faith, who know full well the tenacity of selfish, destructive behavior, and also know the slow but sure journey of grace and healing in our lives. We all have flaws, as Jesus was quick to point out to those who wanted to stone the woman caught in adultery. But in the end we don't help ourselves and cannot lead others forward by denying we have any vulnerability or trying to manage the public fallout by pretending that we are perfect.

Mature leaders not only rely on their strengths, but perhaps more important, learn how to deal consciously with their weaknesses. Through self-examination, they bring their brokenness into the light and turn toward health. Effective leaders learn how to guard against the disintegration of their inward life through dealing honestly with their flaws and vulnerabilities. In contrast to this inwardly attentive perspective, during the impeachment debate President Clinton and his defenders tried to argue that policy is all that really mattered. Judge the president, they urged, on the basis of whether his policies and public actions have promoted justice, worked for peace, and established more fairness in our society. His private life is just that — private — and many seemed to agree. But I believe it is a false and dangerous illusion to hold that public leadership can be segregated from personal integrity. In the end, personal morality and public policy are interwoven, both for a community and for each individual, and the connections between the two cannot be cut. A key task before the political and religious leadership of today's world is to demonstrate the interdependence between society's public policies and the individual's moral actions.

Bill Clinton's wife, Senator Hillary Rodham Clinton, wrote a book entitled *It Takes a Village to Raise a Child,* and the insight of this title is correct. A network of family relationships, voluntary organizations, community and religious institutions, as well as local, state, and federal governmental policies are essential to the welfare of our children. Yet more is required, for kids also yearn for role models to navigate the turbulent moral waters of their lives. But it is not just children who need such models. We all do. So it takes an example to lead a nation — and Bill Clinton initially failed that test of leadership.

In the aftermath of his tardy confession, Clinton did provide a helpful example, which has remained largely unappreciated by a cynical public, by forming an "accountability group" of three pastors — Gordon MacDonald, an evangelical leader who earlier had publicly confessed to adultery and sought rehabilitation and healing; Philip Wogaman, the pastor of Foundry Methodist Church in Washington, D.C., frequently attended by Bill and Hillary; and Tony Campolo, a popular evangelical speaker and friend of Clinton. The media dismissed this group as a canny bit of political theater, but it was, in my opinion, a genuine attempt by Clinton to grapple with his weaknesses and begin to live an examined life. Though these three maintained strict pastoral confidentiality about the content of their discussion, what they could share made clear that the process was real, an assessment reinforced by the fact that they all continued to meet long after the impeachment process had ended. In this group, Clinton modeled what every politician, pastor, CEO, and leader needs — a confidential community of faith and trust, where one's journey, one's wounds, and one's hopes can be freely shared though a well-examined life, mediating the healing power of grace.

Some may think that such expectations are unrealistic, particularly for political leaders, but my experience in Washington, D.C., revealed how possible and essential this is. When I began working on Capitol Hill as a young staffer, it proved difficult to find any church that nurtured my personal faith while also supporting my convictions on the Vietnam War and other social issues. A large evangelical church with an active young adult group was personally warm and nurturing, but almost all its members saw no contradiction between their faith in Christ and their strong support for our policies in Vietnam. An Episcopal church on Capitol Hill, on the other hand, was filled with antiwar activists, but sharing the personal, pietistic experiences of Christian faith seemed uncomfortable and foreign.

I discovered Church of the Saviour, a small and unique ecumenical community founded fifty years ago, which provided a place where my inward spiritual journey could be freely shared and my outward engagement in social issues found strong encouragement. The church was organized around small groups providing a place for each person to share fully his or her personal journey and struggles. Those in the group held one another accountable for each other's growth, in the face of personal challenges, weaknesses, and questions. Further, each group also was committed to an outward "mission" that put faith into action with concrete commitments to justice and service.

Group expectations were high, and weekly meetings as well as daily disciplines of prayer, journal writing, and biblical reflection committed each member to an inward journey toward personal wholeness and spiritual depth. Lives were shared, opened, and gradually but decisively, changed — changed in ways that demonstrated how the power of God's Spirit, over time, re-creates people's lives, healing deep wounds and clarifying the driving spiritual purpose that became firmly rooted in one's being. This experience changed my life and integrated the inward and outward journeys of my Christian faith.

I've also seen prominent politicians involve themselves in groups like this. Certainly that's still the exception rather than the rule. Yet opportunities like this exist for any leader, and those who choose to embark on such a journey find a place and space to acknowledge their vulnerabilities, share personal accountability for their growth, and deepen the spiritual integration of lives and service. In today's world, such qualities are becoming prerequisites for public leadership that can serve effectively and faithfully in the long run.

5

Listening for God's Call

Beneath the challenges posed to any leader by temptations arising from money, sex, and power is a more fundamental question: how does one hear God's "call" for one's life at a particular point in one's journey? At Church of the Saviour in Washington, D.C., I found this language of "call" powerful and clarifying, for the church believes, quite simply, that God addresses each person with a calling, a way his or her particular gifts may be used for building up the church and ministering to the hurts and needs of society.

I have no doubt that God does call us in this way; our problem comes in listening, so that this call can be heard. And I daresay most of us don't know how to listen for that call. We have to learn.

The founding pastor of Church of the Saviour, Gordon Cosby, had been a chaplain in Europe during World War II, and through many dramatic episodes Gordon witnessed how soldiers to whom he ministered lacked the inner spiritual resources to cope with the horrible realities and anxieties presented by war. They were equipped neither to live nor to die. So upon his return to the United States, he and his wife, Mary, were determined to start a church that could nurture the inward spiritual journey of its members, evoke their particular gifts, and equip them for costly service and ministry in the world. To make this a reality, each potential church member was asked to commit to particular activities, the long list of which included fifty minutes spent each day in prayer, Bible reading, and journal writing to develop one's inward spiritual pilgrimage; membership in a "mission group" to which they were accountable for their growth and participation in its outward mission; preparation for membership through a period of study, reflection, and "internship"; the tithing of 10 percent of one's income to the ministry of the church; at least an annual time of retreat; and an opportunity each year to consider whether to recommit to membership or not.

Such a set of expectations hardly seemed like a formula for starting and growing a new church. But now, fifty years later, the ministry of Church of the Saviour has spread throughout Washington, D.C., and has shaped the Christian journeys of tens of thousands throughout North America and the world. Books written by the late Elizabeth O'Connor chronicling the life and growth of the church, such as *Call to Commitment, Journey Inward, Journey Outward, Our Many Selves, Eighth Day of Creation, Search for Silence,* and others, have had a profound impact on countless Christians and congregations.

Today the Church of the Saviour has intentionally divided into several small communities each with a particular focus of ministry. Its fruitfulness has been remarkable and its ministries manifold: Jubilee Housing, a major initiative in inner-city housing; Columbia Road Health Center; Christ's House; the Samaritan Inn; the Servant Leadership Institute; ministry with the homeless; and much more, responding to the needs of those within inner-city D.C., as well as sharing this model of the church with hundreds from across the country who come to visit and learn. But in the end, Cosby would say that all this abundance of service is rooted in the commitment of each of the members to listen for God's call in their lives, and such listening requires the discipline of intentional attentiveness to one's inner journey and to God's presence in their lives.

I have no doubt that God does call us in this way; our problem comes in listening, so that this call can be heard. And I daresay most of us don't know how to listen for that call. We have to learn.

People today need radical structures to enable careful listening to the presence and Spirit of God. As never before, our intellectual and emotional circuits are literally overloaded with constant stimuli — thousands of voices, messages, and images received each day, each one attempting to shape our values, direct our dollars, and influence our choices. Listening for God's call on our lives, in the midst of this environment, requires deliberate, countercultural steps to create inner space. Often this happens by retreating to a place designed for that purpose.

One of the first acts of Church of the Saviour was to buy a farm outside of Washington, D.C., as a place for retreats. Through all these years, that place, called "Dayspring," has served as the spiritual center for the diverse communities spawned over the years, and as one might expect from a church rooted in listening, a retreat at Dayspring centers around silence.

My first encounter with Church of the Saviour came when I was working on Capitol Hill, and I found the model of this unique church curious and attractive. However, the idea of its disciplines — spending almost an hour each day in prayer, reflection, and something called "journaling" — seemed out of the question. As for many others on the "Hill," my work lasted easily seventy hours a week on what seemed like crucial legislative issues. How could I ever find the time for this "inward journey," and what would it mean, anyway? Besides, all these requirements smacked of legalisms. All the same, I eventually signed up for a retreat at Dayspring. Leaving Senator Hatfield's office earlier than normal on a Friday, after a hectic week, I drove out to Dayspring, my mind filled with those things left undone. As an introduction to the retreat we gathered at the Lodge of the Carpenter, where the leader shared some thoughts, and then told this group of fifteen people that we were to be silent for the next twenty-four hours: no talking, no conversation, no radio or TV, no music, no newspaper — just the tranquility of a forest, on the edge of a field, above the Merton pond.

I was stunned and scared. Never in my life had I been silent for that long, especially with other people. For hours my mind simply recycled the events of the day and the past week, the agenda waiting for me on Monday, hundreds of trivial concerns passing across my mental computer screen. Prayer at first seemed impossible. Then gradually, the external silence entered within. I began to become still, to reflect on my life, and to pray. On Sunday morning, we retreatants — who had even shared our meals together without speaking — were invited to "break the silence" and share. The result was astonishing. Deep insights, vulnerable struggles, and dramatic encounters with God began to fill our space as each of us recounted our experiences, and a profound sense of community was created. I listened as people yearned to discover what gifts they had to offer and where God was calling them in mission and ministry. Most of the retreatants were lay professionals, some with government jobs, others in a variety of positions, but all were seeking a spiritual center that would orient their lives around their relationship to God. Absent was any superficial, phony piety. No one was looking for any spiritual quick fix. We knew this journey involved discipline and hard, intentional work, and we believed that inner clarity and the call for our lives would emerge if we did this work.

So I joined this path, deciding to become a member of the Church of the Saviour, setting forth on an inward and outward journey to become more attentive to God's presence, both with me and in the world. I would be listening for God's call. Differently said, my process of self-differentiation was under way.

A couple of years later, I went on retreat to another location, at a Trappist monastery outside Washington, D.C., in Berryville, Virginia. By that time I felt more comfortable with the disciplines required for the inward journey. At Berryville I was graced to have one of those life-changing encounters, when the presence of God's radiant love totally overwhelmed my being and crystallized all of my life's experience in a few defining moments of God's grace. Though words don't easily describe such experiences, lives are shaped by such times, these sacred moments, and so was mine. From then on, my life's directions began to unfold with compelling inward clarity. A relationship dramatically resurrected led to marriage. I left my work on Capitol Hill to join the staff of a new magazine of radical Christian social witness called *Sojourners* and to be part of its supporting community in inner-city D.C. A few years later my wife and I left for Missoula, Montana, to be part of a church community there, starting new work dealing with stewardship of the environment. At the time none of these actions or decisions seemed to make much sense from a practical point of view, and there was often much stress and pain in these risky transitions. But through listening — and hearing — God's call, I was now living my life according to an inner spiritual direction.

People today need radical structures to enable careful listening to the presence and Spirit of God.

Twenty years later, Gordon and I had lunch at the Potter's House, the Church of the Saviour's coffeehouse on Columbia Road in the Adams Morgan neighborhood of D.C. He was now eighty-two years old, and as the Church of the Saviour was dispersed into several new small faith communities, Gordon was guiding one of these, still pastoring. Though we hadn't talked for several years, his very first question was what one might expect: "Well, Wes, how is it going in your inner spirit?"

In our conversation, I asked Gordon if any of his convictions about the church had changed over fifty years, to which he replied, simply, "No." More than ever, he said, people need commitment to a group to nurture their faith, support their inner journey, and evoke their gifts, and they need to become directly engaged in mission, serving the poor. To-day's culture makes it harder to be the church. But it's all the more essential.

Further, it takes rare commitment for the long haul to produce "deep change." Summing up his own ministry, Gordon said modestly toward the end of our talk, "You know, Wes, I feel that I'm only scratching the surface."

6

Defining One's Self

Over the years since my time at Church of the Saviour, I have found that faithful progress on my inward journey, in the midst of demanding vocational responsibilities, is simply hard work. Yet this is essential for a continual process of personal development and growth, and that's a lesson I've had to continually relearn. For instance, during my time serving as director of Church and Society for the World Council of Churches in Geneva, Switzerland, my work was filled with excitement and challenge. I organized conferences with an ecumenical diversity of church leaders, addressing issues like the ethics of genetic engineering and global warming. We gathered participants from around the world in Kuala Lumpur to discuss the prospects for global ecological sustainability and the churches' response. Kinshasa, Zaire, was the site for a conference on the ethics of nuclear energy. For six wonderful years my vocational life was filled with such responsibilities.

Yet those years, in retrospect, were marked by less attention to sustaining my inner spiritual journey. Sometimes it felt as though my inward life was in neutral while my outward work was accelerating faster than ever. I remember a conversation in Santiago, Chile, at a WCC Executive Committee,

with a staff colleague, Myra Blyth. We walked across an ir-
rigated hillside outside the site of the meeting and talked
about what watered our souls in the course of our work.
Some other WCC staff had similar yearnings. In the midst
of urgent ecumenical activism, as we addressed daily the
pressing needs of a world suffering from injustice, racism,
violence, and ecological destruction, time to nurture one's
soul seemed sparse, and almost selfish. Yet all of us need the
replenishment of living waters to participate effectively in
God's work to heal the world.

During those years, I learned that it's hard to pursue
one's inward spiritual journey alone. We need those who
can encourage and guide our journey. When I returned from
Geneva in 1994 to begin service as general secretary of the
Reformed Church in America, I promised to take a retreat
day for prayer and reflection nearly every month, and I decided to find a "spiritual director." This is a term long used
in the history of the church to describe a person who acts as
a skilled companion on the inward spiritual journey of another. Through the ages, those who have taken seriously the
inner development of the soul, seeking what today therapists
might call internal psychological coherence and integration,
never believed this to be an easy task. One's progress along
the path, therefore, could be facilitated with the help of a
skilled companion who has already traveled along the way.

The concept is quite simple. When I go fly-fishing in Montana and want to float the Madison River, I'd much prefer
to do so with a guide, because when I'm accompanied by
one who has floated down the river countless times, he can
chart the way for me. He knows when the water gets turbulent and can sense quickly, before me, when the weather may
turn dangerous. He remembers by which rocks and close to

which banks the trout are likely to be holding. He assists in choosing which flies I should use, depending on the temperature, time of day, and expected hatches of various insects. He even points out what is wrong with my casting technique and how to better present my fly on the water.

In the end, of course, I must do the fishing, and believe me, he has no control whatsoever over whether a trout rises to my fly or not. That seems to depend entirely on the spirit. But my guide can keep me out of trouble, tell me what to expect, and point me in the right direction.

Likewise with a spiritual director. He or she has been down these paths many times before, with lives shaped by thousands of hours of prayer. Some live by the monastic disciplines of contemplation, simplicity, community, celibacy, and worship. Others may be deeply engaged in a life of service flowing from the wellspring of an unquenchable spirituality. But all are trained in the art of caring for another's soul, skilled in the ways of the spirit as a surgeon is skilled in dealing with the vulnerable intricacies of the body.

During those years, I learned that it's hard to pursue one's inward spiritual journey alone. We need those who can encourage and guide our journey.

Over the past decade I have worked with different spiritual directors. One regularly suggested to me various practices and spiritual exercises to assist in my journey. Another shared out of his experiences and questions as he listened to my own. But each spiritual director I have encountered has known how to create a safe and welcoming space where I can come and share deeply out of my inner dialogue to know and listen to God. Those who are skilled in their practice know how to ask the simple, probing questions that cut to the core of my life.

For instance, at the beginning of one meeting with my spiritual director, he asked me a simple question: "What presently is defining your life?" I felt like saying, "My work," because that is what it had seemed like over the previous weeks filled with back-to-back meetings with our governing boards and a weekend retreat with five hundred pastors and their spouses. My director was pointing to the persistent danger of rooting our identity in what we do rather than who we are.

We live in a culture where it seems almost natural for work to define our identity. Think of how quickly, when meeting someone new, you ask what they "do." We subtly assume that the work we do defines us. This pattern of identifying oneself with one's job can be particularly true for leaders, who carry responsibility for the institutions they run day in and day out. Often they become psychologically enmeshed in the organization they help lead, until even their social life becomes an appendage of their work. The tensions of work stay with them in their sleep, so even their dreams are shaped by the immediate drama of their jobs.

Such leaders can be efficient, proficient, and competent, but the danger is that they can fail to give an organization what it most needs because of their inability to foster a healthy and creative detachment from the organization they head. They usually lack the capacity for vision that can decisively shape the organization's future. Rabbi Edwin H. Friedman was one of the most discerning observers of the relationship between organizations and leadership in today's culture. In *Generation to Generation*, he used family systems theory to examine the functioning of churches and synagogues, which in turn led him to broader observations about the dynamics of leadership and society. Before his untimely death he was working on a major book on the subject, and in a video and study guide titled *Reinventing Leadership*, which summarizes his insights, Friedman argues that the most important quality for leaders today is what he calls "self-differentiation." This concept, borrowed from Murray Bowen, one of the founders of family systems therapy, simply indicates one's capacity to chart one's own course in a lifelong process, in which one is emotionally present, but not reactive to others. What does it look like to be "self-differentiated"? Friedman describes certain behaviors:

- Taking a stand in an emotionally intense system;
- Saying "I" when others are demanding "we," or not automatically conforming to keep the peace;
- Containing one's reactivity to the reactivity of others, which includes the ability to avoid being polarized in a situation of conflict;
- Maintaining a non-anxious presence in the face of others fraught with anxiety;
- Knowing where one's own sense of self ends and another person's begins;
- Being able to cease automatically being one of a system's emotional dominoes;
- Being clear about one's own personal values and goals;
- Taking maximum responsibility for one's own emotional being and destiny rather than blaming either others or the context.

These hallmarks of self-differentiation are essential for leaders in today's culture, Friedman argued, because the social context in which we live is marked by chronic anxiety, such that many traits he first observed in families he saw displayed in society as well. High emotional reactivity comes to replace clear discourse: simply witness the over-heated rhetoric dominating politics these days. People who tend to "herd" together into like-minded groups that then do their thinking for them are quick to blame others for problems and find convenient scapegoats rather than accept their responsibility and seek creative solutions. Chronic anxiety creates a "quick-fix" mentality, where easy and superficial answers are given to address complex, long-term challenges. *If leaders give in to the pressure to adapt to these qualities of chronic anxiety in an organization or group, the system cannot help but become even more dysfunctional.* Imagination is thwarted, indecisiveness is accepted, and sabotage is condoned, while efforts to "keep the peace" become a top priority of the CEO, pastor, or administrator.

A "self-differentiated" person, on the other hand, can bring to such a system encumbered by anxiety exactly what is needed for health and regeneration. As a non-anxious presence, such a leader can reduce the threshold of the group's anxiety and make a space for creative action. In not responding to others' reactivity, a leader who is self-differentiated can break the cycle of blame and sabotage. By bringing clarity about principles and vision, such a leader can reorient a group's energy so that it looks outward toward its future rather than remaining emotionally hooked and paralyzed by its internal conflicts.

The task of self-differentiation is not easily accomplished, however. In fact, Friedman once wrote that one never becomes a fully self-differentiated person. "No one ever gets more than 70 percent there," he once said. Nevertheless, developing this quality within the leaders of the churches or synagogues, and of the corporations and universities, is essential to any of those organizations' health and growth.

When I began my service as general secretary of the Reformed Church in America, Jack Elliott, a pastor who had served on the denomination's search committee for this position, handed me a copy of Friedman's *Generation to Generation*. I had never heard of the author and found the book to read like a tedious college text on family systems theory. But as I read further, I came across critical insights into the dynamics of a group like our denomination and found that a whole new understanding of my role as a leader started to emerge. Further, these insights reinforced what I had learned first at Church of the Saviour concerning the necessity of an inward spiritual journey that focused my life through listening for God's call.

Countless times since then I have returned to Friedman's perspectives and found confirmation and guidance. In times of significant tension, I have come to see the transcendent importance of acting as a non-anxious presence when facilitating various tasks. In periods of severe personnel conflict, including painful decisions that need to be made, I am aware that the challenge is to refrain from reacting to the reactivity of others. And in the midst of hesitancy, skepticism, and resistance, I am clear that the overarching task I have been given is to reorient our denomination's energy toward a compelling vision for its future mission. Frequently I have failed these challenges, allowing myself to get "hooked" by others' unhealthy emotional responses or letting myself get overwhelmed by the organization's immediate demands and

tensions rather than maintaining a rooted and centered presence in the midst of institutional anxiety. Nonetheless these
insights into self-differentiated leadership have rung true for
me and their usefulness continually verified.

If "work" is the answer to the basic question asked by
my spiritual director, "What presently is defining your life?"
then we risk becoming so co-opted that, as leaders, we can
no longer offer that objectivity and clarity of purpose an
organization finally most needs for its own health. But if we
are rooted spiritually in our own self-definition, then from
our centeredness we may be able to offer to our organization what is most essential for its livelihood, fruitfulness and
growth.

7

Finding Freedom

If effective leadership is linked as much to internal self-definition as to external behavior, then a clear knowledge of one's personality and psychological make-up is paramount. This is different, though not unrelated, to the discoveries that come through spiritual direction. At times we need to uncover why we are who we are, and in the process may discover psychic wounds in need of healing before an abiding and liberating acceptance of our self can be achieved.

Many in society regard any form of psychological counseling as a stigma, something needed only by those with serious problems. If at all possible, counseling should be avoided, and further, if one has undergone such counseling, or certainly psychoanalysis, that fact should remain hidden, as a sign of some fundamental weakness of character.

Another, less negative view may, however, make more sense for the changing model of leadership in today's society. Several years ago, I recall listening to my friend, the author Elizabeth O'Connor, wonder aloud why candidates running for high political office such as president, governor, or senator, would want to keep secret that they had undergone any psychological counseling. "Why," she asked, "should such a fact automatically be used against someone politically?" She thought it much preferable to support political candidates who had taken the effort to develop a deep understanding of themselves. Since the pressures on such persons are enormous, so similarly is the danger that they might project unresolved inner conflicts onto others and find their political judgment distorted.

Imagine a president, for instance, who is so inwardly fearful of being seen as weak that he feels compelled to undertake an unnecessarily aggressive military response to an international crisis. Think of a senator whose ambition is so driven by an unmet inner need for approval that he or she is incapable of taking an unpopular stand on virtually any issue. Consider a college dean whose painful, repressed wounds from a fundamentalist upbringing create a cold hostility toward any forms of fervent religious expression on campus. Or observe a newly appointed CEO whose paralyzing fear caused by his father's rejection of him as a child now surfaces as he is given authority, rendering him virtually unable to make essential personnel changes.

Too easily, those in positions of responsibility can be dominated by unresolved inner needs that they do not consciously understand and thus cannot monitor and control. So they unwittingly project unrecognized personal wounds or insecurities into the life of the organization. They allow their internal wounds and weaknesses to dominate their external actions in ways they do not fully comprehend.

Those charged with responsibility for giving direction and exercising positions of leadership within an institution, including the task of supervising others, are under an obligation to know themselves. A healthy organization will welcome and encourage such steps. Dick Hamm, formerly the general minister and president of the Disciples of

Christ denomination, and a close personal companion over the years, shared with me his activities on a sabbatical. "I relaxed, played, and did some focused psychoanalysis," he said. Why? Because, he explained, some "inner stuff" was coming to the surface, getting him hooked, and interfering with his responses to various challenges he was facing in his work. So he simply took some time in counseling to address these internal issues. Because of his attentiveness to knowing himself, Dick consistently served as a mature and highly effective religious leader.

I have also found psychological counseling to be helpful in understanding hidden motivations and needs that could interfere with my service as a leader. Several years ago I was given a book, *The Drama of the Gifted Child*, which explored how some children gain their sense of security by continually excelling in meeting expectations of parents and others. In a pattern that starts very early, these children form an identity that is based on performing almost perfectly to fulfill an external image held by their parents, but in the process become alienated from their true sense of self. These insights struck true to my experience, and I worked with a counselor on how to distinguish needs to meet others' expectations from a yearning to discover and express the aspirations of my true self. Then this psychological exploration was reinforced as my spiritual journey focused on listening for God's call at pivotal points in my life.

However much effective leadership is linked to internal self-awareness, in the end, there is still a difference between self-knowledge and a saving knowledge of one's self. Our most basic and often most difficult task in life is not just to know who we are, but to receive what one might call the deeper knowledge of the heart, that awareness that one is fundamentally loved, accepted, and forgiven.

I could explain this knowledge of the heart in both psychological and spiritual terms, but here I prefer to speak as a pastor. Despite our responsibility to work toward deep self-awareness, in the Christian tradition our inner sense of identity and self-definition is not something that we can create but instead is a gift given to us by the Creator. This gift lies at the heart of authentic religious experience and faith. For Christians, baptism is intended as the external sign, or sacrament, of this gift. In our baptism, we are identified as ones who are claimed, called, and accepted by God's love. In spite of all the other forces that attempt to control and define our life, our baptism continuously reminds us that our inner being is being shaped, loved, and redeemed by God.

Christians understand that through acceptance of this gift in baptism, the life lived by Jesus, as God's Son, now becomes the source and pattern of our life. When Jesus was baptized, a voice from heaven affirmed his identity, saying, "This is my Son, the Beloved." This same sense of being God's beloved is the gift offered to us that secures our identity. Accepting this love allows us to know how to answer that question, "What is presently defining your life?" God's love for who I am, and who I am called to be.

In this love we discover true freedom. As long as our identity is vested in what we do, we will forever be vulnerable to the captivity of others' expectations, and we will be subject to the rule of our own needs for self-justifying achievement and approval. If our identity remains rooted in our accomplishments and satisfying others' expectations, we remain as children psychologically and spiritually. We work harder and harder to meet external needs because this gives us our sense of worth, but this never quite succeeds, and in the process our inner self becomes malnourished. That makes us vulnerable to self-gratification, whether through money, sex, food, or other means to satisfy cravings that can be met only by grace-filled love, acceptance, and care. We must nurture our inner self, therefore, not through our outward accomplishments, but by being rooted and grounded in the gracious presence of God's boundless love.

The late Henri Nouwen, in *Return of the Prodigal Son,* summarized what this reality of accepting God's acceptance of us means for those who are called to lead and serve others. "As the Beloved, I can confront, console, admonish, and encourage without fear of rejection or need for affirmation. As the Beloved, I can suffer persecution without desire for revenge and receive praise without using it as a proof of my own goodness." Such knowledge of the heart is the final goal of the journey for any who seek the inner freedom of knowing who and whose they are, and then freely and graciously offering the gift of themselves in their service and leadership of others.

8

Discovering Strengths

As we try to define ourselves, listen for our call, and direct our life's work, a portrait of who we are as persons eventually emerges. For leaders to know who they are as persons is critical, and naturally a variety of helpful tools and approaches can assist in this process of self-awareness. The personnel policies of some institutions and corporations require that a set of psychological tests be given to an applicant before finalizing the hiring of any executive staff, the purpose of which is to discover if there is any underlying serious psychological dysfunction that needs concerted attention and might impair the person's performance. In this approach the focus often is on uncovering potential weaknesses.

A more positive approach, though, would be to provide the opportunity for the individual, and also for that person's supervisor, to look at the particular strengths that characterize the person. The Gallup Organization, for example, has developed highly effective tools that help individuals understand and maximize their strengths. Through tens of thousands of interviews and research, Gallup has identified various "themes" that describe how people function using their talents. A "StrengthsFinder" testing process enables individuals to discover which of these various themes characterize their particular strengths. Leadership seminars and other activities designed by Gallup assist individuals in understanding and applying these insights.*

The underlying principle is simple: Focus your attention on what you do best, and then figure out how to compensate for those areas where you do not excel. If you write with your right hand, don't spend your time and energy trying to learn how to write left-handed. Gallup's philosophy is that leaders and organizations become most effective when all are enabled to discover their particular strengths, and then can be matched — or best of all recruited — for those roles that enable their particular gifts to be maximized.

I've been through this process twice in the last five years, and it's had a profound effect on how I understand myself as a leader. The second time all our directors and senior staff — fifteen of us — went through this process together in a three-day seminar. This has deepened our understanding of one another, significantly enriching our working environment, and since then we've extended the same process to all our staff members.

Through Gallup's extensive research, they've identified thirty-four potential strengths, or themes. These are defined as "a recurring pattern of thought, feeling, or behavior that can be productively applied." Individuals discover which of these themes are their top strengths, as well as which are their weaknesses. I'll use myself as an example. My top five "strengths" are these:

*The background for this material comes from the Gallup Organization, Princeton, N.J., and the thirty-four "StrengthsFinder®" theme names are trademarks of the Gallup Organization, Princeton, N.J. More information about the "Discovery Leadership" and "Living Your Strengths" Seminars can be obtained from Gallup University, 901 F Street, N.W., Washington, DC 20004, or at www.gallup.com.

Ideation: "You are delighted when you discover beneath the complex surface an elegantly simple concept to explain why things are the way they are."

Achiever: "By the end of the day you must achieve something tangible in order to feel good about yourself."

Strategic: "You . . . sort through the clutter and find the best route."

Futuristic: "You are a dreamer who sees visions of what could be and who cherishes those visions."

Communication: "You like to explain, to describe, to host, to speak in public, and to write."

In Gallup's approach, my effectiveness will come in learning how to develop and fully utilize the positive traits that come to me naturally. At the same time, I have to be aware of those themes that describe my weaknesses, such as *Adaptability*, which means "going with the flow"; *Empathy*, or imagining myself in the feelings or situations of others; *Discipline*, which means relying on routine and structure; *Context*, defined as understanding the present by researching its history; and *Harmony*, or avoiding conflict and seeking areas of agreement. In areas like these, I need to develop partnerships with others who possess these strengths so they are expressed within the life of the organization. **My goal is not to be a "well-rounded" leader, but rather to focus on the unique gifts that I can bring, and then make certain that the strengths of others bring all that is necessary — including the things that I lack — to our work as staff for the Reformed Church in America.**

Certainly this gets complex, since in addition to those themes I named, there are twenty-four others that are reflected in sequence according to their relative strength in my own profile. Likewise, my staff colleagues each have their own unique sequence of strengths, and none are identical.

The creativity comes in sharing these, and then discovering how best to work with one another, allowing each of us to maximize our particular strengths, while cooperating with one another in complementary ways. When we entered into this process together, it became liberating and exciting.

Gallup's philosophy is that leaders and organizations become most effective when all are enabled to discover their particular strengths, and then can be matched — or best of all recruited — for those roles that enable their particular gifts to be maximized.

But how do we understand this approach theologically? Especially within the context of Reformed theology, people can get uncomfortable when you keep talking about focusing on a person's "strengths." What about sin? Doesn't any well-grounded, biblical approach begin by recognizing the capacity of every person for self-deception, pride, and egotism? The answer comes first in recognizing what theologians have called "common grace." Gallup's research simply demonstrates that every individual is gifted in unique ways with natural talents and God-given abilities, and that's a theological truth all Christians need to embrace. The effect of sin comes as we allow such strengths — whatever they are — to lead to selfishness, pride, and vainglory, rather than regarding them as the mysterious and wondrous gifts of God's grace in each of our lives.

Moreover, Gallup's approach to leadership brings a refreshing honesty, transparency, and humility to the understanding of oneself. No one is strong and gifted in all ways, and everyone has specific weaknesses. By freely identifying, or even confessing, those areas where we simply are not gifted, we build a community of acceptance, openness, and grace. Being clear and free about one's weaknesses, as well as one's strengths, builds a genuine spirit of mutuality, for we recognize vividly that each of us is deeply dependent upon the other, and everyone's unique strengths and gifts are needed for the health of the whole.

Consider an example of how Gallup's approach has been used within the Reformed Church in America. Like other denominations, one of our major challenges is starting new churches, a complex and crucial process involving a strategic analysis of need, the investment of resources, and leadership. Our experience repeatedly showed that we could pick the right location and raise the money, but the success of the church depended almost entirely on the person chosen to be the founding pastor. Some pastors succeeded while others failed. We wondered why. So we asked the Gallup Organization to help. Pastors who succeeded and those who did not were interviewed in a careful, objective process, at which point Gallup created a portrait or "template" of the kinds of strengths and traits clearly associated with those who had successfully planted new churches.

Now those who believe they are called to begin new churches are put through an "assessment clinic." They are evaluated and compared to the template developed by Gallup, all of which is shared openly with them, though of course other factors in the story of the individual are taken into account as well before a final recommendation is made. The result has been that the percentage of successful new church starts has increased markedly.

Many other tools exist that can help relate personality traits to organizational roles, such as the Myers-Briggs Personality Type Indicator. This widely used test identifies a person's personality traits according to four pairs of personality characteristics: introvert versus extrovert, sensate versus intuitive, thinking versus feeling, and judging versus perceiving. Each person, of course, is a mix of each pair, and not an either/or. But we all have tendencies in one direction or another, and these may change over time or be altered by particular situations in which we need to function on an ongoing basis. But in the end, the test indicates one's dominant personality "type" according to one's tendencies with regard to each of these pairs of traits. Thus, one might be an Extroverted, Intuitive, Feeling, Judging personality (ENFJ), or an Introverted, Sensate, Thinking, Perceiving personality (ISTP). In all, sixteen types are possible.

When a group or team takes a test like the Myers-Briggs together and compares results, it then has another valuable means for understanding many of the dynamics in relationships between members.* Further, different kinds of tasks can be better matched to one's particular aptitudes. Such a tool can also help reveal the particular style for management and leadership that a person will be most comfortable

---

*The first book outlining the theory of these personality types was by Isabel Briggs Myers with Peter B. Myers, *Gifts Differing* (Palo Alto, Calif.: Consulting Psychologists Press, 1980). Since then a wide variety of books has been published on the relationship of Myers-Briggs Personality Type to spirituality, worship, congregational life, workplace dynamics, and organizational change. These include Lynne M. Baab, *Personality Type in Congregations* (Washington, D.C.: Alban Institute, 1998); Nancy J. Barger and Linda K. Kirby, *Type and Change* (Palo Alto, Calif.: Consulting Psychologists Press, 1997); and Sandra Krebs Hirsh and Jane A. G. Kise, *Looking at Type and Spirituality* (Gainesville, Fla.: Center for Applications of Psychological Type, 1997).

exercising. Clearly we know that leadership styles differ according to both the personality of the leader and the culture of the organization. Selecting the right type of leadership style to the need of an organization at the appropriate time of its evolution is critical to institutional health and growth.

Craig Hickman, in *Mind of a Manager, Soul of a Leader,* has developed characteristics of management and leadership styles based on each of the sixteen possible Myers-Briggs personality types. My own "type" will serve as an example. The Myers-Briggs test portrays me as an "INTJ" (Introvert, Intuitive, Thinking, Judging). Some of these traits are stronger on the scale than others. For instance, while I tend toward introversion, I often need to function in extroverted ways, whereas my approach to understanding situations is almost always strongly intuitive. I rely on thinking through issues and will tend toward making judgments rather than simply perceiving different sides of questions.

In describing this type as a "perfecting leader," Hickman says of people like me, "Organized in their approach, they develop long-term and 'big picture' strategies and then work continuously to improve them. . . . Can be perceived as intelligent and aloof. . . . They thrive on an inner world of innovation and possibilities. . . . They prefer anticipating change rather than reacting to change. . . . They are constantly scanning the horizon for a more appropriate and effective structure or approach."

While the above description sounds mostly positive, it's important to recognize that the strengths in each of the four traits also have a downside. If one tends toward introversion, then one needs to do certain extroverted things intentionally, like informally wandering around the office and listening to what's on people's minds. Intuitive gifts can be a real asset, but they can also cause one to not take seriously raw data of the sensation realm. A familiar Myers-Briggs kernel of wisdom is, "A strong 'N' (intuitive) who is a leader needs someone to cover their 'S' (sensation function)." A thinking type's ability to analyze issues should not keep that person from recognizing people's feelings, which might be far more central to arriving at a solution to an organizational problem. A tendency to make judgments, while necessary for anyone in an executive position, should be monitored by the need to perceive all sides of an issue before making a decision.

The Myers-Briggs Personality Type Indicators differ significantly from the Gallup Organization's approach to identifying strengths because they measure different things. Myers-Briggs uncovers psychological predispositions and tendencies, while Gallup is focusing on characteristic talents and natural abilities in one's behavior. For instance, a close colleague of mine serving as a chief operations officer has the same Myers-Briggs type as myself, but we discovered that his top "strengths" as identified by Gallup are completely different from my own, and that we complement each other's strengths and weaknesses in very helpful ways.

A few years ago the Gallup Organization interviewed five thousand executives as part of a study of excellence in leadership. Their discovery was that the most talented leaders reported that their self-awareness, or knowledge of self, was one of the most critical factors in equipping them for leadership. Leaders who understand that they must bring the gift of their own self-definition to an organization, rather than have the organization define them, will welcome tools of self-awareness and use them to understand who they are, and they will encourage their colleagues to do the same.

9

Abusing a Sacred Trust

If the knowledge of one's self is foundational to serving effectively as a leader, what are the dangers of a lack of self-awareness in the lives of those given positions of authority over others and responsibility for an organization's health and growth? A leader's deficit in self-knowledge can damage relations with key personnel and foster a climate of uncertainty and distrust toward his or her decision-making and motivations. *Often leaders who eschew the journey of self-understanding unintentionally invite others to undertake that task for them, and the result is an undermining buzz of speculation, conjecture, and mythology among colleagues about what really makes a leader tick.*

However, other greater dangers — even mortal ones — can threaten leaders who live unexamined lives, exposing their followers to dreadful tragedies. That has been the painful reality made manifest by the revelations of sexual abuse committed by priests and pastors. Recently publicized cases of sexual abuse by priests and the cover-up within the Roman Catholic Church have had devastating consequences for the faithful and their leadership. Apologies and new policies, while beginning to have some impact, have done little to remove the stinging sense of disillusionment and betrayal felt by many, and further, a climate of prevailing suspicion has had a debilitating effect on all clergy, Protestant and Catholic.

In a church there is no more troubling and damaging abuse of leadership than sexual misconduct. The examples are painfully frequent, occurring in mainline Protestant, Orthodox, evangelical, and Pentecostal churches as well as the Roman Catholic Church. Pastors or priests function in a symbolic as well as a personal role with their parishioners; to them, the pastor represents the truths that the church proclaims. In the celebration of baptism and communion and at marriages and funerals, the religious leader speaks the words and embodies the tradition of the church's faith through the ages.

Whether high church or low church, Episcopalian or Pentecostal, pastoral leadership in a congregation represents a reality that transcends the person called to serve in this role. Of course, this leadership doesn't mean that the pastor or priest is beyond human shortcomings. In fact, in a healthy congregation, parishioners will enjoy seeing their pastor protest a close call in a church softball game, or hear a priest mutter familiar words on a fishing trip when a twenty-two-inch trout breaks his line and gets away. But when they are functioning in their pastoral role, they are in a sacred space, and when they function as a listening, supportive presence, they must create an absolutely safe place for anyone to enter in order to confess, share, and find blessing. They are called to transmit the trustworthiness of God's mercy and grace and can do so only as their own lives are experienced as a trustworthy presence by those whom they serve.

When a pastor or priest violates this space through sexual misconduct, this fundamental relationship of trust is shattered. Automatically, such a violation is not just a personal issue between two people, nor can it ever be justified by any arguments of consent. Rather, it represents a betrayal of the larger church's promise to welcome all people with the dependable, accepting, and redeeming love of God. The victim invariably feels violated not simply by the pastor, but also by the church, and consequently even by God. Famous pastors found guilty of such betrayal become infamous, like Jimmy Swaggart and Jim Bakker, but the instances of less famous local pastors becoming sexually enmeshed with emotionally and spiritually needy parishioners create similarly awful paths of devastation. Marriages are ruined, congregations are torn apart, and ministry is mocked.

For pastors in particular, establishing a safe place of trust, whether with such a group or with a spiritual director or counselor, seems indispensable to the practice of trustworthy ministry.

This experience of violation lies at the heart of the emotional anguish and anger felt by those who are the victims of clergy sexual abuse and by the victims' families and loved ones. Legal remedies, financial settlements, and public apologies, while all necessary, are not sufficient to enable a full process of healing. These wounds go deep and require psychological and spiritual responses that transcend what any court can provide.

Such transgressions of leadership make it imperative that every person who becomes a pastoral or religious leader deal consciously with the power and vulnerability of sexuality.

Healthy self-examination and ongoing attention by the pastors to their inner life can prevent such unfortunate damage, whereas inattention will leave one vulnerable. Consider, for instance, the story I know of one pastor who became caught in such a tragedy. When he was young, he was unpopular and unattractive. Most rejected him, or paid little attention. Then, once in pastoral ministry, he found his true gifts and became extremely successful. His preaching was inspiring, his personality was inviting, and his congregation was growing. Suddenly everyone was paying him the kind of attention he had never received before — especially from women. And he just wasn't prepared to handle it. Transgression, pain, and tragedy resulted as he broke his marriage vows and his indiscretions were publicly revealed by those questioning his leadership for a variety of other reasons. The resulting wounds have lingered for long, and damaged many.

Or take another example. Several years ago, an elected president of my denomination engaged in serious sexual misconduct. He also was a gifted leader, with charisma and creative energy for ministry. His congregation was flourishing, and his influence was being felt widely. Then, in a pattern of misconduct and cover-up, it all began to fall apart. When his transgression was discovered and he was finally confronted, he simply left his congregation as well as the denomination, thereby avoiding any process of accountability, and started another ministry.

Several years later, shortly after I began serving as the denomination's general secretary, I received a call from the new pastor of the congregation that had endured this painful betrayal by their former pastor. He asked if my wife and I could join them for a weekend devoted to their healing process, and we did so. Despite the years that had passed, the scars were still very deep, and the congregation was continuing in its struggle to restore its life and health.

As pastors with charisma and energy become successful, with expanding ministries, new opportunities, and constant demands on their time, they can become more vulnerable to engaging in sexual misconduct. Captivated by the apparent success and empowered by the admiration of others, they may not recognize or admit their fallibility in this area, forgetting the testimony of the Apostle Paul, who after confessing his own weakness was told by the Lord, "My grace is sufficient for you, for my power is made perfect in weakness." Such pastors, like any other leaders, need people and places that keep them honest about themselves. Healthy congregations know this and are proactive in encouraging pastors to find a supportive circle of fellowship to share their lives and to take time for nurturing their family relationships, spiritual life, and professional growth.

It's often said of leaders that "it's lonely at the top," and I have experienced how that is true. That's all the more reason why forming intentional relationships of sharing, trust, and accountability is essential. For most of our marriage, my wife, Karin, and I have belonged to various small groups based on a commitment to share our journeys of faith and to provide mutual support for the challenges and questions we all face. For pastors in particular, establishing a safe place of trust, whether with such a group or with a spiritual director or counselor, seems indispensable to the practice of trustworthy ministry. Often in the course of my pastoral leadership I've asked this simple question: "Is there one place where I know I can go and share virtually anything I need to about my journey, and find safety, counsel, and support?"

While the foregoing examples are drawn from churches, the wisdom applies to positions of leadership and trust in other institutions as well, to other relationships where there is an assumption of sacred trust, confidence, and safety: doctor and patient; psychologist and client; teacher and student; lawyer and client. Because of the power and vulnerability inherent in such relationships, appropriate boundaries likewise are vital for them to function in a healthy manner. Any leader committed to the overall health of such institutions will always be steadfast in building an organizational culture that maintains the integrity of such relationships of sacred trust.

Fortunately, within the church, it appears that cases of sexual misconduct are limited to a very few clergy. The vast majority of pastors and priests serve with faithful integrity, as demonstrated by the research that has come in the wake of the devastating scandals of sexual misconduct within the Roman Catholic Church, involving numerically only a relatively small number of priests. Healthy pastors and priests do the inner work necessary to deal with their sexual vulnerability and build integrated personal lives. They need encouragement to take the time necessary to replenish their inner lives, so that God's grace may continue to flow through their ministry.

10

Changing
Organizational Culture

The *Harvard Business Review* featured an article entitled "Changing the Way We Change." Its authors, Richard Pascale, Mark Millemann, and Linda Gioja, contend that while many corporations are undergoing widespread changes in their structures and programs, a deeper level of change is needed and sought. Such "revitalization or transformation" they say, "is what more and more companies seek but all too rarely achieve." The goal of such change is "a discontinuous shift in organizational capability — a resocialization so thorough that employees feel they are working for a different company" ("Changing the Way We Change," *Harvard Business Review* [November–December 1997]: 128).

Three very different organizations that had worked effectively at such fundamental change were examined in the article — Sears, Roebuck and Company, Royal Dutch Shell, and the U.S. Army. In each case, the authors found that "the 800-pound gorilla that impaired performance and stifled change was culture." The ability to clearly reshape the "culture" of the organization was fundamental to enabling change and revitalization.

In attempting a definition of what is meant by corporate culture, the article suggested monitoring four "vital signs" of the health of any organization:

1. *Power.* Do employees believe they can affect organizational performance? Do they believe they have the power to make things happen?

2. *Identity.* Do individuals identify rather narrowly with their professions, working teams, or functional units, or do they identify with the organization as a whole?

3. *Conflict.* How do members of the organization handle conflict? Do they smooth problems over, or do they confront and resolve them?

4. *Learning.* How does the organization learn? How does it deal with new ideas?

The temptation is to believe that a change in corporate culture is largely a matter of correcting organizational structures, devising clear planning, and prioritizing the allocation of resources. While all those measures are necessary for correcting "organizational drift" and charting a clear course, they alone do not ensure that more basic changes in the habits and ethos of the organization will occur. Often these are the changes that are essential if the organization will sustain its journey on the course it has set.

The best example I have to share is the one closest to home. Serving as the general secretary of the Reformed Church in America, I've learned that denominations are complex organizations often with well-established cultures. Our particular denomination, for example, dates its history in the United States back to 1628, which means that its established ways of functioning have been shaped by a long and rich tradition. Used in this way, the term "culture" can be defined simply as "the formal and informal ways in which people relate to one another." Or, in one of the six definitions given in Webster's dictionary, "behavior typical of a group or class." Our culture in the Reformed Church in America has evolved, of course, in the context of the changing American society; yet distinctive features exist that can describe the Reformed Church's "culture." For instance, we respect and expect good preaching. We value teaching and learning. We take intellectual life and theology seriously. Our church government is well developed, with an emphasis on order and orderliness. We affirm collegiality and corporate responsibility, and we hope for moderation and tolerance. We attend to business thoroughly and well.

Obviously, with almost a thousand congregations influenced by a wide diversity of backgrounds and settings, these features of our culture don't characterize every single expression of every church, but they do characterize the shared ways of functioning that we use when we gather in denominational assemblies and governing bodies. In the Reformed Church in America, we come together regularly in these larger groups to govern the various parts of the denomination's life and ministry, and the assumption is that such assemblies meet to transact business, serving generally as legislative bodies, thereby fulfilling a necessary and important function in the overall life of the denomination. Yet this assumption can too easily reduce denominational gatherings to routine business meetings, and because our "culture" values orderliness, deliberation, and thoroughness, we know how to turn such business meetings into tedious experiences of parliamentary debate and micro-management by committee.

Often absent from such meetings are opportunities for personal sharing, building community, listening to each others' stories, discerning vision, open-ended listening for God's direction, and exploring together new directions for common mission. In short, the style of our meetings is captive to our particular denominational culture, and that culture is too restrictive in what it normally permits, encourages, and expects.

So our challenge has been to find ways in which our culture itself can be reshaped and renewed. As is the case with Sears, Roebuck or Royal Dutch Shell, the changes that are necessary in the Reformed Church in America to enable faithfulness to our mission and calling in the future will not be possible without changes in our organizational culture. One first step was simply to create space within our assemblies to go about our work in a new way, starting with the General Synod Council, a sixty-member board meeting three times a year with a business agenda each time the size of a telephone book. Instead of our usual process, we decided to take one of the meetings, set aside the agenda entirely, and gather together having read the book of Acts from the Bible as our only preparation. This shifted the focus to reflections on how we, as a denomination, understood our sense of mission in the world, drawing comparisons to the experience of the early church as recorded in Acts. Such a new way of meeting together was a hard adjustment for some members, and we found ourselves in new, and somewhat unfamiliar territory. With time, however, we began to learn how to relate to each other in fresh ways, sharing more freely in reflection and prayer, listening more openly, and beginning to imagine the possible future shape of the denomination.

Three such retreat sessions, over three years, were required for the General Synod Council to begin to reorient its focus, function, and style. In the process, the members increasingly saw that their role was, in the words of the organizational consultant John Carver, to "look up and out, not down and in." In so doing, the council approved a sweeping statement of mission and vision for the denomination and began to take ownership for how that would be implemented.

This governing body of the Reformed Church in America has continued to evolve and experiment as we try to settle comfortably into a new style and culture. But by starting with creating an open space and permitting other styles of interaction that members wanted but felt constrained from implementing, we established a path of organizational renewal. We began to change the way we change.

Changing organizational culture can often begin most easily on the periphery of an institution, where spaces can be made to experiment with new approaches, model different ways of behaving, and incubate examples of innovation. After all, the values and style of an organization's culture change more through practice than preaching, with the result that such change comes like yeast in a loaf. A little bit of leaven can enliven the whole organization. Or, to use a modern metaphor, a modest alteration to an organization's "DNA" may enable it to grow and shape its life according to reformulated and different expectations. Eventually, though, changes within an organization's culture must move from the periphery and become embedded in its primary structures.

In the denomination I serve, this meant changing the style and process of the General Synod, the annual meeting of the denomination and its highest governing body. Centuries-old traditions had formed the style of this event, and in many respects it had always functioned well. The careful work of preparation, the rules for procedure, the structure of its committees, and the process of deliberation seemed to be an effective way to do the business of the church.

Yet that very effectiveness also was precisely the issue, for the meeting was always structured around business. Times for worship and social activities were always planned, but the point of the gathering was to make juridical and legislative decisions, reinforcing the sense that the business of the denomination was, as Calvin Coolidge might have put it well, business.

However, our delegates came with other hopes, and these expectations always showed up on their evaluations. They wanted fellowship, a unique chance for them to experience the wider life of our diverse denomination. Indeed, for many delegates, a General Synod was the first and perhaps the only experience of meeting with so many others in the Reformed Church in America from across the country and around the world. So delegates strongly valued the times set aside for worship. For many, it was deeply moving to sing, pray, hear preaching, and share in communion with so many others, so much so that a large number typically said worship was the most deeply meaningful part of the week. Further, some delegates came with big questions on their mind, wondering about the future direction of the denomination. They wanted to have a better understanding of why their congregation was linked to this family and what money sent to "denominational headquarters" paid for. They asked how the Reformed Church in America was responding to the challenges of mission and ministry in a rapidly changing world. Unfortunately, despite such hopes and expectations, the main focus of these delegates' time and energy was legislative sessions, going through thick workbooks, and voting on hundreds of recommendations that they might not even fully understand.

The structure had another unintended effect. It automatically elevated any item of controversy and conflict into the center of the General Synod's attention. Thus, a common question before coming to a General Synod would be, "What are we going to fight about?" Would it be homosexuality? Or abortion? Or a theological statement on mission among Moslems? Or full communion with the Evangelical Lutheran Church? It did not matter whether such issues were the most crucial concerns facing the ministry of our 945 congregations, nor even decisive matters shaping denominational priorities for mission. The process ensured that, if any matter was controversial, it would generate major attention. Now if the structure and procedure of a meeting are designed principally to settle disputes in an orderly manner and make efficient decisions, then people naturally assume that such disputes and decisions are the most important matters before the organization. Further, a process focused on conflict also naturally centers attention on voices in either extreme. Yet studies of denominations and other groups demonstrate that most members hold more moderate views, and resist being pushed into those extremes. The challenge, in the midst of a process set up primarily to deal with polarized conflict, is to give voice to this moderate center that often is the real, though silent, majority.

In restructuring our General Synod meeting, therefore, to resolve such culture-based problems, we began to change the focus. For instance, by introducing a theme for common reflection and challenge, such as "evangelism in a changing world," we began to draw time and attention toward important questions confronting us all. We experimented with building into the schedule of our business different Bible study approaches and small group interactions. We scheduled forums on issues of concern where delegates could come to talk, listen, and learn rather than debate and vote. In one General Synod, worship was made a focal point, which enabled us to incorporate the riches of song and style from churches around the world. In this way, delegates shared insights and experiences about the rapidly changing styles of worship today, an issue effecting nearly every congregation in North America.

Because such changes were well received, in 2000 we attempted a risky and bold experiment. Our General Synod met that year in New York City, and after doing preliminary business, we suspended it, inserting instead a gathering called Mission 2000, to which every congregation was invited to send someone. About twelve hundred people came from throughout the country and were placed in "engagement groups" going out to experience the exciting city ministries happening throughout New York.

Along with such encounters within the city, those attending Mission 2000 gathered in worship celebrations to hear inspiring preaching from Emilio Castro, former general secretary of the World Council of Churches; James Forbes, pastor of New York's Riverside Church; Robert Schuller of the Crystal Cathedral; Arthur Caliandro from the historic Marble Collegiate Church; and others. Then in "discernment groups," delegates together listened to what the Spirit was saying to our church about our calling and mission. Because all this took place on the weekend of Pentecost, the forty discernment groups, through an innovative and well-devised process, shaped a "Pentecost Letter to the Churches," subsequently distributed to all our congregations. Only then, following these inspiring three days, was the General Synod reconvened.

Needless to say, the tone and style of that synod were dramatically different. Mission, global and local, was placed at the center of our collective concern. Potentially divisive issues found resolution. A spirit of common purpose transcending various differences was clearly in evidence. But most important, the participants in Mission 2000 from around the country and the New York area churches had a transforming experience. New bonds of connection were formed, and fresh vision for the mission of congregations today was instilled.

Our experience at the 2000 General Synod was not unique. In religious organizations today, national assemblies are being altered through creative experiments to meet the challenge of how to blend together celebration, the building of community, the casting of vision, and concrete needs for decision-making. Richard Hamm, former president and general minister of the Disciples of Christ, puts it this way. "Leaders of the World War II generation try to effect change through organizational restructuring. Leaders of the Baby Boomer generation try to do so through changing the organization's culture." The religious organizations today equipped to address the dramatic challenges posed by North American culture in the twenty-first century are those that have intentionally learned how to instill steady and deep change in their organizational culture.

11

Instilling New Values

Max DePree is a corporate executive who understands well how essential it is for leaders to give focused attention to the culture of the organizations that they serve. Before his retirement, he served as CEO for the Herman Miller Company, which became known not only for its high quality office furnishings, but also for its innovative practices and policies on behalf of its employees. DePree in particular gave constant attention to the values and ethos of the Herman Miller Company, continually seeking to engage the company in a broad understanding of its context and mission. He has shared his wisdom and experience in three influential books, *Leadership Is an Art, Leadership Jazz,* and *Leading without Power.* They each demonstrate an acute awareness of the task of leadership today and the dynamics that shape the intangible qualities and cultures of organizations.

In *Leading without Power,* written especially with not-for-profit institutions in mind, DePree lists "attributes of vital organizations." As opposed to what one might expect from a distinguished corporate CEO, DePree lists elements such as truth, access, discipline, accountability, nourishment for persons, authenticity, justice, respect, hope, workable unity, tolerance, simplicity, beauty and taste, and fidelity to a mission. Clearly one can't program and structure most of these intangible, if not transcendent qualities, but DePree suggests that an effective leader can and should nurture them in the life of an organization, thus shaping its culture.

Building sabbath time into the routine of our daily schedules is a continual challenge and runs against the grain of attitudes and values in our society.

Max DePree is not only a member of *Fortune* magazine's National Business Hall of Fame, but is also a faithful member of Third Reformed Church in Holland, Michigan, a congregation of the Reformed Church in America. Further, he has served on the board of Fuller Theological Seminary and other church-related groups. So DePree's insights into leadership do not stem simply from his forty years of experience in the corporate world. Rather, they flow from his persistent attempt to integrate his mature religious wisdom and faith with his knowledge of dynamics of organizational culture, be they profit or non-profit groups, universities or local elementary schools, hospitals or hospices, corporations or denominations.

How can such changes in the culture and values be instilled into its life of an organization? Altering the style and focus of governing board meetings and assemblies, as I have presented, is one approach. Yet such a change involves only those delegated to participate in these official bodies. Cultural changes in that venue may be essential, but such shifts in culture also almost by definition need to go beyond, to permeate the wider life and membership of an organization.

Non-profit groups as well as some corporations confronted with the need for transformation are asking this question. They wonder, for instance, if we spend hundreds of thousands of dollars to gather our constituency, or our members, or our employees together, what then should we do with this opportunity? How do we use such occasions not just to transact the business of our governance or share information but transform the fabric of our organizational culture?

One radical approach is to call members together intentionally and not do any business or press any specific organizational agenda, but rather simply come together to celebrate a common community, provide a space for personal renewal, and connect people to the organization's guiding mission and vision. The results can be surprising, healing, and enriching. Our denomination attempted an experiment something like this a few years ago, having realized that the normal reason that the denomination hosted a national meeting was to promote some organizational agenda. Indeed, pastors, who carry out the daily work, mission, and ministry of the denomination, frequently feel that the national structure is preoccupied with selling a program, requesting funds from their congregation, or promoting some new initiative in need of their support, and their feelings, we saw, were not unfounded.

So one year, instead, we invited pastors, and their spouses, to a "Spring Sabbath," on the weekend after Easter for a time of rest, recreation, and renewal. The event was designed as a way to say thank you to the denomination's pastors and make room for the gift of friendship, fellowship, and worship with each other, free from any other obligation or expectation. A speaker was chosen on the theme of "sabbath" and entertainment was arranged, but much time was also left free. As we looked forward to the event, I must confess that we really didn't know what to expect.

The response to this experiment was heartening. Hundreds came, and we realized, in fact, that this had been the largest gathering of our pastors ever assembled in one place in our entire history — worshiping, relaxing, renewing friendships, healing old wounds, sharing stories, and finding encouragement for their service. When the evaluation forms were tabulated, we saw that rarely had any denominational event been so deeply appreciated and praised. Two years later we repeated the event, with a similar result.

We had tapped into the important need for sabbath rest and renewal that often is a deficit in the lives of pastors as well as many others. Jesus modeled this practice in his own ministry, as seen in passages like Mark 1:35, "In the morning, while it was still very dark, he got up and went into a deserted place, and there he prayed." In planning for Spring Sabbath, we used a similar text as our theme: "The apostles gathered around him, and told him all that they had done and taught. He said to them, 'Come away to a deserted place all by yourselves and rest a while.' For many were coming and going, and they had no leisure even to eat" (Mark 6:30–31). That seemed to picture the lives of us as pastors; we are so busy with our "doing" that we neglect giving attention to our "being."

Building sabbath time into the routine of our daily schedules is a continual challenge and runs against the grain of attitudes and values in our society. Most organizations implicitly value those who put in the longest hours and constantly fill the available spaces in their lives with more work, and those expectations can easily take hold in religious institutions as well. But Jesus demonstrated a far more centered approach in his ministry and life, practicing regular time of withdrawal for prayer and not allowing the fervent expectations of others to eliminate the time he and his disciples needed to be apart for prayer and renewal.

So for us, this Spring Sabbath — a gathering *not* centered on business or program needs — was one attempt to shift our organizational culture, and in my estimation it met with success. Those who gathered had an experience demonstrating that the gift of our fellowship together was far stronger than issues over which we may differ, and pastors received a space for their personal renewal and encouragement in ministry that came through the initiative of their denomination.

These lessons appear relatively simple, and my guess is that many corporations are far ahead of religious organizations in understanding the importance of thanking, affirming, and serving those who are its key distributors, or franchise operators, or dealerships. Healthy non-profit associations understand the vital importance of nurturing, affirming, connecting, and thanking those who are its local representatives or leaders of grassroots chapters. These more person-centered values become even more important in the future as the information revolution continues to change the way knowledge is shared and communication takes place.

In a high-tech world, people need a high-touch culture where they live and work. The kinds of values and qualities identified by Max DePree need to be experienced by the employees, sales representatives, local agents, pastors — whoever holds those key, close-to-the-ground responsibilities for carrying out the organization's mission. Those people must feel they are being served and genuinely valued by the organization rather than simply being expected to serve it.

12

Deciding How We Decide

Central to the culture of any organization is its means of making decisions. Any group, association, family, company, church, football team, school board, or fishing club has to have some agreed-upon way of making choices and reaching decisions. The process may be explicit and formal or implicit and informal, but any group develops a decision-making process and style.

Complex social organizations normally formalize their decision-making process in procedures, rules, and by-laws. In reality, a wide variety of forms and styles of decision-making is possible for complex groups to function cohesively. However, most modern organizations assume that a straightforward parliamentary model with clear rules of debate and majority vote is the only viable or fair method to employ.

Models that parallel those of parliamentary institutions also govern most American religious denominations. Representative bodies are established, drawn from geographical regions. Delegated members meet in a deliberative process governed usually by Robert's Rules of Order. Matters are debated, and votes are taken. Decisions are made by majority rule. For these religious bodies, the assumption is apparently that God's will can best be discerned through the opinions of 51 percent of those present.

But the church, of course, has not always governed its life by majority votes in representative legislative bodies governed by Robert's Rules of Order. A rich history of various forms of governance and decision-making has been largely neglected. In the "conciliar" tradition, special councils met for extended times of discussion, prayer, debate, and resolution of crucial issues. The task, at its best, was not to forge a slim majority of votes but to discover together a way forward that most agreed represented the truth. The foundational example of this tradition is the Council of Jerusalem, described in the New Testament in Acts 15 and referred to elsewhere. Some parts of the Christian tradition have been guided by a process of consensus, or more appropriately, seeking for the "common mind" of the group. Such approaches assume that a highly conflicted and polarized situation resolved through one side narrowly prevailing over the other is not one likely to produce a sustainable course of action that is truly led by the Spirit.

At points in its history the church has placed more emphasis on spiritual discernment than on political deliberation in guiding its life, more attention on listening to each other in a common search for God's leading than on argumentation and debate. Techniques for such spiritual discernment have been well developed in some traditions, just as rules for debate have been in the more parliamentary systems, but most mainstream American church cultures that run along the democratic model are simply not as familiar with discernment or consensus techniques as a way to function. I do not pretend that there are easy answers for decision-making processes of religious bodies — or secular organizations either. But a range of alternative processes exists within the Christian tradition and can be explored.

Charles Olsen, a Presbyterian pastor, has been a pioneer in this direction for some time. His small book *Transforming Church Boards into Communities of Spiritual Leaders* (Washington, D.C.: Alban Institute, 1995) provides a way to think freshly about how meetings can be conducted according to a framework different from the customary opening prayer and plunging into the agenda. Many boards of local congregations as well as other levels of decision-making bodies are working with Olsen's model. Often called "Worshipful Work," this approach incorporates storytelling about the past and present experiences of God's action within the body, biblical and theological reflection on major themes that are faced, discernment around important decisions, and visioning for the future.

Olsen joined with Danny Morris, a Methodist, to write *Discerning God's Will Together.* This is a substantial exploration into various approaches to decision-making and governance, and maps out the specific movements and steps that constitute a discernment process. A true process of discernment, in their view, moves through "framing, grounding, shedding, rooting, listening, exploring, improving, weighing, closing, and resting." Specific questions and suggested techniques accompany these steps, and they chart a process for any group to follow that can result in a more rooted, accepted, and discerned outcome.

When Olsen had just finished writing this book, I invited him to meet with a group of senior staff of the Reformed Church in America to begin a dialogue about whether and how such a discernment process could be utilized within any of our own governing structures. Slowly, we began to experiment, starting with a question about how best to alter our own staff organization, and how to change my job description as general secretary, to best focus our efforts on the mission facing the denomination. The process took time but worked well, enabling changes that could have been quite contentious to occur in ways that gathered widespread confirmation.

Then we invited Chuck Olsen to assist in guiding a major discernment process at Mission 2000, enabling the twelve hundred people who gathered to discover a common message to give to the wider church. Forty discernment groups with trained leaders met to reflect on their experience and pray, while "sages" were identified who gathered the wisdom of these groups and shaped it into a "letter" that was then presented to the General Synod and shared with every congregation. The process was remarkable and far different from the typical attempts I have known to draft statements emerging out of large church or ecumenical assemblies. The letter resonated with a depth of language and spiritual insight and was affirmed by the participants at Mission 2000 as reflecting their wisdom.

Following that experience, the General Synod Council decided to use this discernment process to formulate a ten-year goal to embody our sense of where God was calling us in future faithfulness and fruitfulness. We worked in small groups, moving through the steps as outlined, over a year's time, and reached a final plenary with a proposal. Rather than vote in a normal manner, each member was given three cards — green, yellow, and red — and through the discussion the moderator took the sense of the group on various issues; green cards meant affirmation, yellow cards meant one had reservations but could agree, and red meant one was strongly opposed. Time was running short, and we were stumbling through this new process, realizing that while we had probably two-thirds or more in favor, several members still had serious reservations. So we decided to wait on a final decision and take another year.

At the time I remember feeling frustrated and nearly frantic, for my clear expectation was that we should have moved this proposed goal forward. In a normal political process, this would have been possible, but it would not have been wise. Taking more time meant we were giving integrity to the discernment process we had embraced and were willing to trust this process even when it led in directions we had not anticipated or desired. The additional time led to new and valuable insights as well as far wider dialogue throughout the denomination, so that when it was finally brought to General Synod for a clear decision, in yet another discernment process, the delegates were able to embrace a refined version of the ten-year goal with unanimity.

Various church bodies are taking up the challenge to change the decision-making process of their organizational culture. Among the most interesting is the World Council of Churches, which recently made a commitment to use a consensus form of decision-making in its governing body, a 150-member Central Committee. For the WCC, this decision emerged from three years of focused and intense discussion with the Orthodox churches in its membership.

Because severe tensions between the Orthodox churches and the WCC had surfaced prior to the Harare Assembly in 1998, a Special Commission was formed, made up equally of representatives from Orthodox and other member churches of the WCC to address a set of serious concerns. As one who was serving on the Central Committee and previously had been a member of the WCC's staff, I was asked to serve on this Special Commission. The tensions addressed by the commission grew from a perception by many Orthodox that their perspectives and sensitivities were not being taken seriously within the WCC. In discussions of controversial social and ethical issues and in the practice of worship and prayer, the Orthodox frequently felt marginalized.

One of the overriding Orthodox concerns was the system of governance and decision-making used by the WCC. Though made up of about 325 member churches from every part of the world, the WCC's governing style has followed a Western parliamentary model. Central Committee members sat at desks piled high with documents and reports. Issues were debated, motions were made, and the majority ruled.

For the Orthodox churches, as well as for others such as indigenous churches in Africa, this parliamentary style of decision-making was a foreign way of conducting church business. In practical terms, the Orthodox were concerned that a 51 percent majority could decide crucial issues affecting the life and witness of the churches in the WCC, but beyond this concern, they worried that their presence and voice, accounting for a significant portion of the WCC's membership, could not be fully received and heard within such a style of governance of the WCC.

They weren't alone in their reservations about the WCC's decision-making ethos and methods. Once formed, the Special Commission took up this concern and began to draw on the varied experience of its member churches. The Uniting Church of Australia, for example, had been using a system of consensus decision-making for several years, and in its assembly had devised means for testing or discerning the sense of the house in the midst of its discussions. Instead of bringing matters to decisive and divisive votes, the general direction of the body is ascertained and alternative courses of action are then considered, after which the body seeks to move forward as much as possible in ways that gain the consensus of its membership. All this had been well developed in rules of procedure outlined in detail by the Uniting Church of Australia.

Other experiences as well were studied by the Special Commission, such as the methods used by Quakers to discover the common mind and leading of the Spirit in a group. This process over three years led the Special Commission to propose that the WCC's Central Committee move toward making most of its decisions in consensus style. Procedures are being devised, and a period of learning has been established, but this global, highly diverse ecumenical body has embarked on a major transition into a new style of decision-making for its governance.

In the three years on the Special Commission working on the issues creating tension between the Orthodox and other churches, I saw clearly the need for creating a safe space where listening and sharing could occur free from dynamics of public political debate. Stereotypes between the Orthodox and others needed to be broken down, and a climate of authentic fellowship needed to be created. This required careful attention not only to our formal agenda, but also to the venue, style, and spiritual climate of our meetings. We found avenues to encounter one another at the level of our common commitment to Christ, doing so by discovering ways of changing the culture of our meetings.

As various religious bodies explore ways of utilizing discernment and consensus in their governing style, they are drawing both on ancient wisdom and modern insight into group process. *In the years ahead, changes in decision-making processes may represent some of the most fundamental shifts of organizational culture, especially for institutions governed by representative bodies.* Changing the way we make decisions may be the most critical step in changing the way we change.

13

Asking the Big Questions

Walter Brueggemann is a renowned author and scholar of the Old Testament whose perceptive insights into the imagination of the prophets and the contemporary relevance of the wisdom in the Hebrew Scriptures have awakened many to these timeless resources. We had not seen each other in years when we sat down for lunch at an ecumenical conference in Hungary, and as I might have expected from a prophet, we had barely exchanged greetings when he said to me, "So you're the general secretary of the Reformed Church in America. Do you have time to ask the big questions?"

Prophets know how to get right to the heart of the matter, and Brueggemann certainly did with me in my work. His question is the one that someone should ask every CEO of any organization at least once a week, for anyone who has the task of being a leader, and not simply a manager, must find a way to place those "big questions" before the organization's staff, governing board, and constituency, effectively and consistently.

The "big questions" bring into focus the central purpose, or driving force, of an organization. A corporation asks, "What business are we in?" A hospital asks, "Who are we serving?" A liberal arts college asks, "What are we educating students for?" Such foundational questions seek to clarify an organization's "mission," a term itself with a long religious history as well as a meaning in diplomatic and military fields. "Mission" suggests a gathered group, called to move in a clear direction, guided by a desired outcome. "Mission" is impossible unless it is defined, understood, and accepted.

Another "big question" is what could or should the future look like if an organization is faithful to its mission, issues such as, "Where are we headed?" "What do we want to see changed?" "How will things look five or ten years from now?" "What are we hoping to create?"

In more religious terms, a church or denomination asks, "Where is God calling us?" "What does this promised land that God is calling us to look like?" "What is the shape of the future to which God's mission in the world beckons us?"

"Big questions" seek to clarify a "vision" that inspires, motivates, and energizes an organization. Some outstanding historical examples of providing vision come to mind. Think of Martin Luther King's "I Have a Dream" speech before the Lincoln Memorial at the height of the civil rights struggle — a profound statement of vision, inspiring, in that case, a whole national movement. Vision is rooted in imagination — the prophetic imagination of the prophets, for instance, or the inventive imagination of an Alexander Graham Bell, or the diplomatic imagination of Woodrow Wilson or Dag Hammarskjöld, or the geographical imagination of Christopher Columbus, or the political imagination of Thomas Jefferson.

In religious life, vision is always connected to the work of God's Spirit. Vision is "inspired," meaning that it comes *to* us and not merely *from* us. Thus, in biblical stories, the Spirit speaks through the prophets. God's Spirit calls forth

Abraham to a new land and uses Moses to lead the people out of bondage and into the Promised Land. When Jesus began his public ministry by announcing a vision of justice, liberation, and healing taken from Isaiah, he first says, "The Spirit of the Lord is upon me" (Luke 4). In his ministry Jesus continually offered metaphors, stories, parables, and word pictures of what God's intended future would like and where it already was beginning to appear. Peter, as recorded in Acts 10, was gripped by a vision from the Spirit in a dream of the radical embrace of Gentile and Jew in the community of the early church. He saw a startling picture of animals held in a sheet coming down from heaven and a voice telling him to eat, even though his tradition forbade him from eating unclean meat. A voice said, "What God has made clean, you must not call profane," and Peter embraced the radical vision "that God shows no partiality," shaping a new community in which there would be no distinction between Jew and Greek, slave and free, male and female, for all are one in Christ.

Simply put, vision means seeing something according to the way we believe it should and will turn out, creating a compelling and sustaining picture of our most desirable future. Religious vision roots this in the promises of biblical faith, using what theologians would call "eschatological imagination" and discerning the ongoing movement of God's Spirit within the world beckoning the community of faith to respond. All vision, therefore, comes in pictures and images rather than in mere words and rhetoric. All the lines may not be neatly drawn in, but a sustaining vision will have an attracting, compelling power that will cause people to ask, "How do we get there?" "How can we best carry out our mission?"

In the past decade, organizations, institutions, and corporations have been giving increased attention to clarifying their mission and articulating their vision. "How to" books on the subject are easy to find on bookstore shelves dealing with business and management, and it's no longer unusual for corporate executives, university administrators, and members of non-profit boards of directors to find themselves on a retreat pondering a proposed mission and vision statement. In fact, after a severe storm a few years ago tore through northern New Jersey where I lived, causing some damage to our property, the adjustor from our home insurance company who came to settle the claim handed me his business card, on the back of which was a statement of his company's mission and vision.

Simply put, vision means seeing something according to the way we believe it should and will turn out, creating a compelling and sustaining picture of our most desirable future.

What accounts for this emphasis on mission and vision in the world of today's organizations and businesses? The internal dynamics of American institutions have been changing rapidly and dramatically in the past several years in response to what has been called "the information revolution." Access to information is sharply altering patterns of authority, governance, leadership, and decision-making, and traditional structures of hierarchy and chain-of-command authority, rooted in the control of information, are proving

obsolete, making the coordination, communication, and fa-
cilitation of information a key organizational necessity. In
fact, a whole new vocabulary within organizational life has
arisen. We speak of "networking," "processing," and "ac-
cessing information," creating "systems" that build "synergy"
and increase "capacity." Such language itself, taken from the
field of electronic communications technology, is indicative
of how the functioning of all organizations is changing in
the information age.

In this new environment, naturally, the role of leadership
is likewise shifting. Organizations and their staff encounter
an ever-increasing proliferation of all kinds of information,
which needs to be sorted, interpreted, and evaluated, and
then utilized, stored, or discarded. The flow of our own personal e-mail is a microcosm of what is happening to every
organization.

*In short, we all are faced nowadays with a need to grasp
the difference between information, understanding, and discernment, such that effective leadership should enable an
organization to gather information, interpret what is most
significant, and avoid being distracted by what is interesting
but ultimately insignificant, so as to discern what actions
need to be taken as a result.* This requires clarity of mission
and an imaginative vision for one's future.

14

Casting Vision

In today's information-saturated environment, an organization needs to articulate its reason for being and its primary aspirations. Clarity on what makes it distinctive as an entity empowers movement, driving the mission and the vision in the life of the organization. By understanding the need for a "gestalt," or a guiding, interpretive framework, organizations can then "process" all the information at their disposal, utilizing what is necessary to more toward their desired future and discarding what is not. Nowadays organizations as diverse as the Eddie Bauer Company, the American Red Cross, and First Reformed Church of Pella, Iowa, need fresh, effective ways to link their members or employees and to encourage their creative participation in achieving its purpose.

Today people vote with their hearts. Tomorrow their actions follow accordingly. Therefore, loyalty to an organization is built by clarifying the purpose and meaning for someone's participation. A recent issue of *Fortune* magazine devoted a section to "the 100 companies people most like working for." One of the qualities cited consistently was the ability of a company to connect its mission to the work and contribution of each one of its employees. In the long run, people are less willing to volunteer or contribute because they are told to, because they ought to, or because they are required to. Rather, they yearn to be inspired to participate, to be connected to a process that invites them to offer their particular gifts.

While this trend toward clarity of vision in the service of greater participation is finding wide expression in businesses and other institutions, it is particularly important for religious bodies, where a sense of cohesion, community, and common mission needs to be rooted in inspiration and vision rather than any kind of coercion. Instead of relying on shrinking traditions of institutional loyalty, many denominations, congregations, and religious groups have been listening and working hard to clarify their particular mission and discern the vision they sense God is calling them to fulfill.

The Disciples of Christ, for example, adopted its Statement of Identity, with a declaration of mission imperatives and a statement of the "ethos" of their denomination, prepared by its "vision panel" and including a section on "structural imperatives" and "core strategies." All this eventually led to a clear and concise statement of vision, namely, "To be a faithful, growing church that demonstrates true community, deep Christian spirituality, and a passion for justice" (Mic. 6:8). A few years ago, the United Church of Christ adopted a major declaration entitled "Statement of Commitment — Toward the 21st Century," with vision and values to undergird its programmatic life and leading to major restructuring of the denomination as a whole. Likewise, the Reformed Church in America worked for two and a half years to adopt its Statement of Mission and Vision.

In all of these cases, the purpose is the same: in a time of intense information saturation, with voices constantly competing for our attention and options spread before our membership, some religious organizations have understood the familiar saying that "the main thing is to keep the main thing the main thing."

Today people vote with their hearts. Tomorrow their actions follow accordingly. Therefore, loyalty to an organization is built by clarifying the purpose and meaning for someone's participation.

For the Reformed Church in America, agreeing on a state-ment of our mission and vision was no easy task; this was not a normal part of our "culture," but it rarely is for an organization like ours. Any institution that is 375 years old tends to assume it has figured out its mission and purpose.

However, through a deliberate, often bumpy, and surpris-ing process, we eventually adopted our Statement of Mission and Vision. It begins with a two-sentence statement of our mission: "The Reformed Church in America is a fellowship of congregations called by God and empowered by the Holy Spirit to be the very presence of Jesus Christ in the world. Our shared task is to equip congregations for ministry — a thousand churches in a million ways doing one thing — fol-lowing Christ in mission, in a lost and broken world so loved by God."

Then it provides a picture of vision intended to por-tray what a denomination transformed in this way would look like:

OUR VISION

Imagine . . .

Laity and pastors unleashed, hungry for ministry; inviting, mission-minded congregations, authentic and healing, growing and multiplying, alert to the opportunities around them.

Imagine . . .

Classes and synods as communities of nurture and vision-accountable, responsible, sustained by prayer, alive to the Spirit.

Imagine . . .

A denomination, locally oriented, globally connected, that prays in many languages and beholds the face of Christ in every face; a denomination renewed and renewing, raising up leaders, always directing its resources toward the front lines of ministry.

Imagine . . .

Hurts being healed, the lost being found, the hungry being fed, peace healing brokenness, hope replacing despair, lives transformed by the love of Jesus Christ.

Imagine . . .

The Reformed Church in America, engaging the world.

The statement goes on to say what it would look like to move in these directions, in a third section titled "Living out the Vision":

This vision will be lived out . . .

*By congregations focused for ministry — creative, confi-
dent, healing, and radically attentive to the world outside
their doors.*

*By consistories selected more for ministry than management,
attuned to the Spirit, eager and equipped to serve.*

*By ministers of Word and sacrament open to dream,
prepared to lead, willing to risk.*

*By classes that are empowering and proactive, living in
communion, each accountable to all, and all to Christ.*

*By synods and staff that funnel resources to the local church,
and keep us connected to the larger church.*

*By all the people of the RCA, a network of relationships, a
fellowship that celebrates its gifts and confesses its failures,
and where the ministries of all are valued and cherished.*

*To live out this vision by consistories, classes, synods and
staff, our decision-making will be transformed by a pervasive
climate of worship, discernment, and biblical reflection. We
will no longer do business as usual, nor our usual business.*

In this paragraph we suggested some of the changes in
organizational culture that would be required to move in
these directions, and no phrase was more controversial than
the last line, "We will no longer do business as usual, nor our
usual business." Some heard this line as a negative judgment
on the rich heritage of the past. In fact, one distinguished
retired missionary upon reading the draft sent an impas-
sioned letter to the General Synod, pleading that it all be
redrafted, lest the contributions of the past be neglected.
But at General Synod, other voices argued that they were

not dishonoring the past. Rather, they simply felt they were declaring that their style of meetings and decision-making — the organizational culture — would have to change if they were to live out their mission in the future, and this more forward-looking view prevailed. Because of the adoption of this statement, we've undertaken major new initiatives, and people feel they have been given permission to try fresh approaches as we try to "equip congregations for ministry."

But the real story is how we arrived at these words and the commitments they entailed. Our governing board had been working for almost two years on this process, looking into the future, clarifying directions, and asking probing questions. They had come up with drafts we hoped would be finalized, but they didn't fully satisfy everyone's aspirations. So at the end of a board meeting, they suddenly instructed me to take what had been done and go off on retreat somewhere and craft this into a compelling and final proposal. As one board member put it, "Go up to the mountain, take a few others with you if you want, and let us see what you hear." It was a stunning and unexpected mandate. In accepting to do so, I told the board and staff that if we did this, "Everything would be on the table," a comment that caused no end of heightened staff anxiety.

So I invited seven others from across the country whose wisdom, I felt, would be invaluable, and we literally went up to the mountain, to St. Benedict's Monastery in Snowmass, Colorado. There we entered into the worship life of that community and stayed together for three days of prayer, sharing, crying, and hoping as we tried to turn our hearts, our eyes, and our ears toward God's desired future for the Reformed Church in America. Then the images, metaphors, and words began to flow.

On the last night I had a startling dream, with the image of an executioner's axe and the message that I had to be prepared to sacrifice anything required, including my job as general secretary, in order to follow the mission and vision that was emerging with clarity in the midst of those crystal skies, chanted prayers, and starry nights. I shared this with the group the next morning; we all sensed that this whole process was about far more than phraseology. Never had I felt so vulnerable in my work, for we knew there was significant risk in honestly believing that we had heard a mission and vision infused with God's Spirit that could challenge and change our denomination. It was scary. But we were deeply convicted that this was right and that we needed to be faithful in offering, affirming, and trusting the fruit of this time. When we brought the proposed mission and vision statement back to the governing board, they listened intently, shared enthusiastic responses, and almost spontaneously began singing the doxology.

Words matter. Phrases facilitate. Images invite, especially if they indicate critical directions to be taken and paint a persuasive picture of the future. As the philosopher Seneca said, "Without a sense of direction, it is impossible to tell a good wind from an ill wind." Organizations today will drift to and fro, tossed by every changing wind, unless and until they clarify what they are about and where they want to go.

15

Time, Participation, and Trust

While words and phrases have power to transform an organization, the process in composing them can determine whether such words will be heard and followed or ignored and discarded. Any organization deciding to define or even reformulate its mission and vision needs to build three crucial elements into its process: time, participation, and trust.

Time. This work, if done well, simply takes time, and it should. Images are like seeds that need the right conditions of environment, soil, and time to germinate. Thorough discussion can prepare the soil, and sometimes letting the ground intentionally rest for a while will free up new creativity. **The most common mistake is to assume that this work on mission and vision can be done quickly.** I once was asked to meet with a group of pastors and elders from a local area who had sent out a questionnaire to each of their churches and gathered for an evening to write a mission statement. We had rich discussions together that night, but if they wanted a lasting result, they needed to set aside a year for their drafting process rather than an evening.

Intentional time for the process is essential. A retreat for staff or board members, special meetings devoted just to this task, and readings, videos, or other input can focus the mind and stimulate the imagination. Further, the work of the organization has to go on while its mission and vision are being clarified. Testing and sharing directions and drafts with various groups in an organization is necessary and takes additional time. So the rule is not to rush. I have learned that those involved in the process will tend to have a clear intuitive sense about when they have arrived at a statement ready to be adopted.

Participation. Who should be involved as the primary participants in such a process is a far more difficult question, requiring clarity about who is most responsible for articulating an organization's defining center and for expressing its central aspirations for the future. Let me illustrate the complexity of the question. Who should write a college's mission and vision statement? Its board of trustees, who have ultimate responsibility for the institution? Its president, who runs the institution administratively? Or its faculty, who are the key to carrying out its mission. Should its students be involved? Or take a large non-profit organization involved in alleviating hunger and promoting development around the world. Should its staff define its mission? Or its CEO? Or its board? Or even its donors?

These questions do not yield simplistic answers and will differ according to the various types and structures of organizations and institutions. One starting assumption can be affirmed, however. The president or CEO of an organization must always play a central role in such a process, and in fact, articulating the mission and vision should be a key element in a president's responsibilities within the organization. If he or she chooses to delegate this task to another group and doesn't actively participate, one of two things is likely to happen: either the whole process of vision creation will be undermined, or the chief executive will be disempowered. At the same time, such a process should not be the sole responsibility of the organization's leader, for exclusivity is equally dangerous. It can cause a mission and vision statement to be seen simply as the CEO's brainchild and not really belonging to the organization as a whole.

Any organization deciding to define or even reformulate its mission and vision needs to build three crucial elements into its process: time, participation, and trust.

In most organizations, this process should deeply involve its governing body or board, but here, too, another question arises: how does such a governing body function and understand its own role? This question is particularly pointed in institutions that, in reality, are staff-driven (i.e., faculty driven, doctor driven, etc.), and whose governing boards have become largely rubber stamps chosen for a variety of political or financial reasons. The temptation in such situations is to simply delegate the task of articulating the vision and mission to staff, but that choice has its pitfalls. Can staff detach themselves sufficiently from their programs, responsibilities, and institutional power in order to quest honestly to define the organization's central purpose and most important future directions? Statements of mission, vision, and values written with a calculated political eye to protect vested staff interests and crafted more through political compromise than prophetic imagination will never refocus an organization's energies around a central guiding purpose.

The process of articulating an organization's mission and vision at times may force an organization to clarify the roles of its governing structures. One person who has worked most perceptively on the nature of boards in this regard is John Carver, and in his extensive writing and consulting on his "policy governance," he believes boards should get out of the habit of micromanaging, of interfering in personnel matters, and of undermining the appropriate responsibilities of key staff. Instead, he pushes for organizations to empower their boards to focus on major policy issues, define the desired future of the institution, establish basic directions, and set a framework in which staff can then function.

The president or CEO is usually the key person to initiate a process defining an organization's mission and vision, and, as stated, this should be a part of his or her job description, but a governing board should be deeply involved in the process, especially in the case of religious and other non-profit institutions. Granted, the result may create new expectations for them and change their role. Similarly, staff must be consulted throughout the process in meaningful ways that take seriously their input but don't place inappropriate expectations on them to ultimately control the outcome.

Trust. The underlying level of trust or mistrust within an organization will have a major effect both on the time it takes to formulate a mission and vision statement and on the patterns of participation in this process. In some cases, tending to the culture of a dysfunctional organization (or congregation) is needed even before a mission and vision process can be attempted. Once begun, such a process is likely to reveal where mistrust within an organization runs the strongest.

Those who don't have confidence in the organization as a whole or who are wedded to keeping things the way they are will be likely to resist a process that begins intentionally asking the big questions. Here, a chief executive needs to be particularly attentive. Leadership always has a pastoral dimension, and a wise leader will learn how to draw those with such reservations into the dialogue, while keeping the process clearly on course.

A few years ago, I participated in a gathering of denominational staff executives in a retreat with Roy Oswald, a consultant from the Alban Institute, which offers a wide range of services and resources for congregations and pastors. Oswald asked each of us to analyze how we spent our time in our jobs. He gave us five categories: management issues; training and development of others; ceremonial functions and duties; pastoral care, including conflict resolution; and "spiritual leadership" including discerning the times, clarifying vision, and interpreting our mission. For most, management and conflict resolution took up the majority of our time. Oswald's advice, based on long consulting experience throughout the church, was that the last category of "spiritual leadership," including the defining and sharing of vision, should take 40 percent of the time spent by any effective leader.

I regularly experience that tension in my own work. When my time is consumed almost entirely by organizational management and conflict resolution, I begin to become inwardly depleted. While such responsibilities are an important part of my work, if they push to the distant margins the task of developing others and the challenges of spiritual leadership, I begin to lose the reserves of excitement, joy, and inspiration that are essential for my service. Keeping these roles in balance is not only essential for the health and future of an organization, but also for the vitality and engagement of its leadership.

In most organizations, change and transformation simply cannot be initiated unless their leaders begin intentionally and persistently to ask the "big questions" of vision, mission, and values. Prophetic imagination should never be considered an organizational luxury or a bothersome irritant. It takes a clear choice and an intentional commitment of time and energy, and it is the key, I believe, to any organization's capacity for renewal.

16

Change Is Messy

An organization that decides to define its mission and vision nearly always knows intuitively that it needs to change. The assumption of its leaders is that such change can be planned, managed, and orchestrated in a predictable, organized fashion so most leaders bring the gifts of optimism and confidence to the advent of change. They believe the changes will go well. And they are almost always wrong.

At the outset, the process is always exciting. A long and arduous process has finally produced a crisp, convincing statement of mission and an inspiring expression of the vision for the organization's future. The governing board has given its resounding approval. A video is produced to interpret this new sense of direction for the constituency. Affirmation flows. Hope rises. And then people begin to realize that things may actually change.

At that point, two kinds of anxiety typically arise within organizations. The first is a nagging fear that in the end, despite the fine words and rhetoric, nothing in the organization will ever really change. But second is the destabilizing anxiety over the fact that indeed, everything — yes, actually *everything* — will change.

The plain fact is that transition and change create anxiety, and this anxiety is part of the human condition. Think of how you felt as a child when your family moved, and you entered a new school. Imagine your feelings the first day you began a new job. Remember how you felt when you left home for college. Most of us don't welcome change. We have to leave behind old securities. We are no longer able to predict what will happen. We have to give up trusted and supportive relationships. We lose our previous place, and we become uncertain about what the future will hold. Organizational change may not seem as dramatic as some of these examples; it may be more evolutionary. Yet it can be profoundly destabilizing in ways that both leaders and participants had not anticipated.

In my own vocational experience, I have participated in a variety of organizations, churches, ecumenical structures, and boards faced with the prospect of significant change. All involved intended that the process of transition would go smoothly. But in each case, the real change was messy.

Some twenty-five years ago, the Church of the Saviour faced a number of problems caused by its growth. The sense of community and belonging to the whole was being stretched beyond its limit. Expectations of others for the role of its founding pastor, Gordon Cosby, were becoming impossible to fulfill. He and others sensed that the church could not simply continue to expand its ministries and mission without some fundamental change in the structure. So a group was commissioned, appropriately called the "New Land Committee," to seek a vision and path to the future. Robert Greenleaf, author of *Servant Leadership* and an organizational consultant, gave the group some beginning advice. He counseled us to rely on the founding values and traditions of the community — for example, the notion of the inward and outward journey, the practice of reflection and retreat, our focus on calling forth gifts, and the use of these traditions as tools to guide our process into the future.

The committee worked for a year and concluded with a working retreat where periods of silent reflection and prayer were interspersed with dialogue around the text of a final proposal. The plan called for re-creating the Church of the Saviour into several autonomous communities, each with its own leadership, worship life, and particular mission but linked together by common practices and a coordinating council. The experience was memorable, for it was the first time I had been part of a committee assigned with a task that went about its work in a fashion that integrated so deeply values of silence, prayer, and a listening process of reflection, as well as focused and sometimes contentious discussion, in achieving its result. It demonstrated a spirituality of group process that stood in stark but promising contrast to the styles of political decision-making I was accustomed to in my role as an assistant to a U.S. senator.

The proposal for the "New Land" was embraced with enthusiasm and celebration. Then, as we moved toward implementation, confusion and anxiety began to rise. Who would lead these new communities? How would people decide where to go, and which to join? What would happen to the broad experience of community that we enjoyed? How could we give that up? What about longtime friends who might join a different community? And what about Gordon? How could we survive without hearing his preaching every Sunday?

The pastoral task suddenly became enormous. People's fear, mistrust, and doubts all began to erupt, and, of course, to feed on one another. Some turned their frustration toward Cosby, feeling he was abandoning them. I remember during this time Gordon once said to me, "The problem with being a leader in the church is that when people want to shoot you, they don't aim for the heart. They just try to shoot you in the knee to cripple you." In other words, people don't have the courage to oppose you completely and forthrightly but rather try to subtly undermine your capacity for leadership.

But Gordon and other key leadership stayed on course because he is, I think, one of the best examples of a "self-differentiated leader" I have every encountered. He remained in touch with people's feelings and fears but was not captivated by them. The plan moved forward, and gradually most people became settled in their New Land.

The Reformed Church in America faced similar difficulties in its organizational journey. After the Statement of Mission and Vision was enthusiastically adopted by our highest governing body, we began working with our General Synod Council on its implementation. We made some progress but ultimately found that we had more questions than answers. Then, at an annual staff retreat, anxieties began to surface overtly. Staff didn't have real input into the mission and vision statement; they wondered who was listening to them and were unclear where it was going. They sensed changes were coming but didn't know what that would mean for them. The unexpected departure of a senior staff member further fueled people's anxieties. Some felt they just needed to "hunker down," keep their head low, and do their job. And as general secretary I came in for criticism. Could staff be safe and free to disagree with me? Was I too remote and insensitive to their concerns? Did their voice count?

Two months later the General Synod Council met again, and I gave a report suggesting seven goal statements for implementing the mission and vision statement. However, what was ordinarily a brief executive session without staff ultimately lasted the entire morning, as myriad questions erupted in a free-wheeling, spontaneous discussion. Why were we working on these goal statements? What's the process? What's our role as a governing body? What's our responsibility for personnel matters? How are staff feeling? Where is the mission and vision statement supposed to take us? How should we run our meetings?

The plain fact is that transition and change create anxiety, and this anxiety is part of the human condition.

In short, our institutional commitment to embark on a course of change had triggered anxiety, raising real questions about roles, functions, and process. Careful steps were required to gather together these questions and address them all before we could move forward. But at a personal level, this organizational anxiety was deeply disconcerting. I hadn't anticipated it, and coming after the deeply affirming and spiritually powerful experience surrounding the drafting of the Statement of Mission and Vision the previous spring, these events threatened to throw me inwardly off balance. This was the most serious test I had faced in learning how to lead without defensiveness but with an inner spiritual clarity of purpose.

We made a commitment to listen carefully to one another. Staff members were invited to share their concerns privately with trusted colleagues who were not their supervisors and who had been appointed specifically for this purpose. This feedback was then collected and brought to our next three-day staff meeting. We asked a consultant to work with us in that meeting to help discuss matters together in an open, facilitated process. The result was agreement on specific ways to move forward, including changes in our organizational culture. We were beginning to identify the values we needed to share as we moved forward in our journey.

So what did we learn from these events, and those of many other organizations going through similar experiences? First, we should not have been surprised when, at the time, some of us felt blind-sided by unexpected anxiety and conflict. When an organization initially embraces a compelling vision for its future and embarks on this journey, it generates excitement, affirmation, and hope. But once into the process, tensions, doubts, and anxieties invariably begin to surface. Second, as John Kotter, professor of leadership at the Harvard Business School and the author of Leading Change, puts it, among the eight stages of creating major change within organizations, "creating a guiding coalition" is a necessary task early on. Looking back on the experience in our denomination, we failed to create a "guiding coalition" within the staff at first to carry the vision and its strategy. Our focus was placed on generating strong support and ownership from our governing boards, and though we succeeded there, our staff felt left behind.

As one staff person said, "Since the statement was drafted by a small group of insiders, it does not energize me." It took us a full year or more to circle back and gain meaningful ownership of this mission and vision by most of the staff, so that in time, we began to hear another sort of comment: "I have been part of the staff for sixteen years. But until we entered into the ongoing process of adopting, living into and out from the Statement of Mission and Vision, it was frequently difficult to see how what I was working on supported or related to an overall plan for ministry and mission in the RCA."

Another place we failed was in not sufficiently communicating our vision once it was adopted. Formal approval is only a first step. Kotter says that most organizations vastly *under*-communicate their vision, and in my experience, he is right. We in the RCA eventually saw the need to develop a proactive communication strategy to share the mission and vision statement throughout the denomination. And finally, we learned the essential need in a time of change for identifying and nurturing shared values that shape organizational culture.

So the lesson is this: mission and vision are not enough. As important as they are, they alone won't sustain the journey. Members of an organization also need to be clear about the values they will take with them to shape their culture and life, for people go more easily to somewhere new if they know that values and ways of behavior that they respect will be upheld and even strengthened. Often a process of clarifying an organization's mission and vision will also include an identification and reaffirmation of its central values. This step is crucial for guiding the process that implements the mission and the changes that occur.

In some secular organizations, talk of "values" is not always favored. For instance, in *The Visionary Leader*, a book written for business enterprises, authors Bob Wall, Robert

Solum, and Mark Sobol use the term "guiding principles" and propose that these be drafted along with a mission statement as part of the overall vision statement of an organization. In their framework, "The Mission Statement sets goals; the Guiding Principles shape the culture necessary to achieve those goals."

However, regardless of the language used, as an organization sets off on a journey driven by a mission and inspired by a vision, it also needs to have a shared and respected set of values that all ascribe to. It's a frequent mistake to overlook this process, or assume that such values are clear. In particular, members of congregations and religious organizations may be likely to believe that sharing the same faith automatically means that we share common values. Yet often the opposite is true. Values in this sense are not abstract ideals, but rather qualities that describe our ways of behavior and our treatment of one another as we carry out the mission of the organization. Conflict is virtually a given once an organization commits itself to a clear mission and a compelling vision for its future. Shared values, openly acknowledged and affirmed, become the threads that weave the fabric of organizational culture, enabling it to deal successfully and creatively with such conflict. In times of high tension and stress that accompany such a journey, those values will nurture trust in a process that otherwise seems filled with risk and uncertainty.

17

Creating a Road Map

Statements of mission and vision need to be undergirded by common values and followed by clear goals, objectives, and strategies. To simply have in mind a beautiful picture of where we're headed is not enough. We also need signposts along the way that can check and measure our progress, and those should be laid out on something like a road map.

Some might devise a "strategic plan" for this purpose. I believe it is important not to get too detailed too quickly. Various events and developments will emerge as you move along the road. As with a literal road map, we might be starting in Chicago and traveling to Seattle, but we don't have to plot every stop for gas and food before we begin. On the other hand, we would want to set some goals to govern the trip — say, five hundred miles a day. In the same way, an organization needs to have goals that can be measured, and give some indication that it is moving toward its vision. To do so, staff teams will work on specific strategies and steps to implement the goals.

Expect the road to be bumpy. You can map out a process and time-line for change on paper that looks very smooth and straightforward, just like plotting a route on a road map. To drive a group from Chicago to Seattle looks easy. But what about the sixty miles of road construction on I-94? What about the tornado in North Dakota? Or the transmission fluid leak in the middle of Montana, fifty miles from nowhere? Or a passenger's motion sickness?

In organizational change, the most careful planning carried out through the most sensitive and shared process is essential, but this care alone will not enable a smooth transition. There are too many variables for anyone to control, and many of those have nothing to do with plans on paper; they are rooted in human emotions, which are simply part of life and speak of both the joy and pain that is the gift of every human community.

The saga of the difficulties in making a journey to a new land is as old as the children of Israel. Moses led them dramatically out of their bondage in Egypt and across the Red Sea, with Pharaoh's armies drowning behind them. Believing that their God would deliver them and lead them to a new future, they headed for the Promised Land. But they encountered the wilderness and responded with faithlessness. People began grumbling and questioning, wondering where they were going. They didn't like the food and resisted all this change. They asked why they had left, and even wished they were back in Egypt. Then they questioned whether Moses could be trusted, and in the end, their journey ended up taking forty years.

Allow some passengers to disembark. The painful reality is that not everyone actually wants to go to Seattle. Some really would rather stay in Chicago. Insisting that they go on the trip can make everyone else miserable. Organizations moving toward implementing a statement of mission and vision may have some very discontented members. Everyone should always be invited to be part of the journey, and every leader should begin with the conviction that each person can make the transition and has something valuable to offer to the process. Yet if individuals simply feel that they have no place in this new land or don't really believe in the destination or have deep doubts about the mission itself, then spending limitless energy constantly trying to get them on board may not be wise. Everyone may feel more comfortable, including the individuals themselves if a gracious and affirming way is found for them to disembark.

Change speed but not direction. Organizational journeys have to be responsive to the dynamics of the group. The most important task for leaders is to try to navigate and keep the journey on course. At times the process can speed up, and other times it should slow down. For instance, our group going from Chicago to Seattle may want to make seven hundred miles one day but only three hundred the next because of a visit to the Lewis and Clark Caverns. An organization's periodic ownership of its mission and vision along the way and a reaffirmation of its values are crucial. It's a serious mistake for leaders to always push ahead, or keep rigidly to a time-line. Leaders need to remember that they have probably internalized the mission and vision far deeper than other colleagues, staff, or board members, and therefore, others may have very valid reasons for adjusting the implementation process.

Don't stop to discuss changing the destination. Your group has decided, through a respected and clear process, to go to Seattle. Don't stop in Bozeman and start discussing whether you should go to San Francisco. Get to Seattle first. It can be a great temptation for an organization to go back and tinker with its mission and vision. For some members, it's more fun to keep discussing and refining such statements than to actually try to implement them. But once an organization has made a decision about mission and direction, keeping momentum moving forward toward that vision is crucial.

In organizational change, the most careful planning carried out through the most sensitive and shared process is essential, but this care alone will not enable a smooth transition. There are too many variables for anyone to control, and many of those have nothing to do with plans on paper; they are rooted in human emotions, which are simply part of life and speak of both the joy and pain that is the gift of every human community.

Of course, periodically an organization should revisit such statements, if only, in part, to allow new staff or governing board members to make them their own. Given the pace of overall change in society, some argue that such a process of redefining a vision should happen as frequently as every five years. But the main point is for an organization to keep clearly on course when it is implementing new directions and not get sidetracked by taking up questions that have already been answered.

Vision without strategy is like faith without works: it's great to be inspired, and it's wonderful to internalize what is most deeply true, but all of this must result in changed behavior. This happens best when we understand that vision — like faith — is never an end in itself. Rather, it initiates a journey that heads us in a clear direction toward a desired destination.

Make decisions — don't postpone them. An organization in the phase of implementing change automatically will encounter a greater number of decisions at a faster pace than an organization that is basically stable in its structure, definition, and mission. To continue the analogy, consider everything you have to think about, anticipate, and decide when your car is moving as opposed to when it's parked. Organizations that remain "parked" may seem comfortable, but they get passed by and eventually lose their sense of purpose and direction. When you're moving in the journey of change, people in all levels of the organization need to be equipped to make decisions, and to do so fairly quickly. Postponing and deferring decisions simply slows down the whole journey. Obviously, implementing such change may mean that patterns of authority and decision-making may have to be altered and further decentralized.

Sometimes, in the process, difficult and radical decisions have to be made in order to keep integrity with the commitment to do what the mission and vision statement promise. Finding the way to make those decisions rather than prolong them is always better in the long run, because delaying simply increases the overall level of anxiety in the organization. Most of us, when in a process of institutional change, would rather have clear decisions made about the directions we are headed, even if we disagree, than have decisions put off in ways that only increase our level of uncertainty and apprehension.

However, this wisdom is not always clear to leaders, and so putting off hard decisions in the hope that somehow they may become easier is a common temptation. Usually such decisions don't become easier, and this is particularly true regarding personnel issues. Recently I talked with a former leader of a denomination who had just finished eight years of creative and effective service, and I asked him what in retrospect he would have done differently. His immediate reply was, "I wish I had made necessary key staff changes sooner." That's a common response of many leaders, particularly in religious organizations when they reflect back on their experience.

Nothing has more power to block forward movement to implement a fresh sense of mission than major personnel conflicts in senior leadership of an organization. Change requires cohesion and trust among those who share central responsibility for an institution or group. Severe conflict at that level will tend to paralyze the rest of the staff or membership, regardless of how inspiring its mission and vision may be.

Sometimes you must simply drive by faith. A rental car I once picked up came with a Global Positioning System. I was at O'Hare Airport in Chicago, headed for a destination I had not previously visited, about fifty miles to the south. So I decided to use this directional system. I entered the address where I needed to go. And a small computer map and voice prompt began to give me instructions as I began to drive. "Proceed south on I-294. Prepare to make an exit. Take next left. Proceed on I-55 west. Move into left lane. Exit on exit ramp to stop light," etc.

I found the experience fascinating. I knew where I wanted to go, and I had confidence that this GPS could direct me, but I didn't know all the details of how I would get there. The only clarity possible was one mile and one turn at a time. My arrival depended, not on my detailed knowledge of a map, but on my faith in this GPS system. Luckily it got me there, on time.

Sometimes driving by faith is exactly what the experience of leadership is like. We know clearly where the organization intends to go, and we have trust in a staff, structure, and decision-making process that can get us there, but we don't know the exact route, and we often can't predict very far ahead. The best we can do is stay with the process, day by day, and encourage others to do the same.

Often you have no choice but to live by grace that is sufficient unto each day, which can be very humbling and healing. Especially for those who work with religious institutions and faith-based organizations, living day-by-day reminds us that finally we are not in control. Living into our vision is not achieved by our competence and mastery but rather by our faithfulness to discern daily how we are being directed toward our destination. We need nothing more than faith that the Spirit is present and has already gone ahead of us. The writer of Hebrews says it this way, "Now faith is the assurance of things hoped for, the conviction of things not seen" (Heb. 11:1). That chapter goes on to describe how the key figures in the story of the children of Israel — Abel, Enoch, Noah, Abraham, Sarah, Isaac, Jacob, Joseph, Moses, Rahab, David, and Samuel — lived and acted according to this kind of faith. Like the children of Israel, we are given enough manna, or daily bread, each day to lead us forward, and that is all we need for the journey.

A non-anxious presence. Those with leadership responsibilities are perhaps never more tested to the fiber of their being than when anxiety, doubt, and acrimony begin to engulf an organization that, in fidelity to its mission, has embarked on a process of change. At this point, the organization most needs the leader to be a non-anxious presence, calm in the midst of a storm, sympathetic to fears, but confident of direction.

One thinks of the image of Jesus. Sleeping in a boat being tossed by winds and waves, and awakened by his anxiety-ridden disciples, he calls them to faith as his presence calms the storm.

Leaders need to remember that they have probably internalized the mission and vision far deeper than other colleagues, staff, or board members, and therefore, others may have very valid reasons for adjusting the implementation process.

In a transitional period, leaders frequently must also learn how to absorb the pain people feel. Any group will tend to vent their frustrations, apprehensions, and anger onto its leader, and such a psychologically symbolic role is almost inevitable for one who carries final responsibility for any organization. Mature leaders have learned how to discern and accept this reality, and they are able to break the cycle of emotional reactivity that can so paralyze an organization by absorbing the emotion without retaliation. In other words, they "play through the pain" like athletes who do what is necessary for the team despite their own discomfort. Such leaders do not overreact or take themselves out of the game: they will keep focus on the welfare of the greater group. They accept and openly acknowledge valid criticism but deflect emotional "cheap shots" so they lose their sting. They serve the whole organization by reducing collective anxiety, maintaining clarity, and opening space for others' creativity.

The fact that change is messy can probably not be avoided, but it need not be wounding or destructive. Rather, it should be an occasion for creativity, excitement, and hope. A key to making it so is leaders who have the gift both to stay the course and to stem the fears of others through a trusting confidence rooted in their souls.

18

Leadership Styles

As the pace of change in society continues to accelerate, all organizations are facing the pressure to determine how they must adjust, renew, and alter themselves, sometimes in radical ways, in order to remain viable. Above all, the complex, messy nature of change requires gifted leaders to guide these organizational journeys, and this need for quality leadership accounts in large part for the explosion of attention, concern, study, and analysis of leadership over the past couple of decades. When I went to Amazon.com and used "leadership" as my search word, 6,004 hardcover books and 13,994 paperbacks were offered in response — all this in a market that, I venture to say, is still not saturated.

Our society is hungry for wisdom about leadership because people feel the need, every day, in their workplaces, churches, government offices, and voluntary organizations for authentic, inspiring leadership. Too often they find it lacking. Remember Mayor Rudy Giuliani in the aftermath of September 11, 2001? He did what a leader facing such a massive tragedy ought to do — give the people of his city clear information, demonstrate resolute commitment, and provide hope through his words and actions. Under his leadership, New York and New Yorkers were able to face an unprecedented disaster and mobilize to rebuild and heal.

For such transformative service, Giuliani became a national hero. His past controversial activities and combative personality were quickly forgotten because he demonstrated a capacity for leadership in that crisis. A year later his book, entitled simply *Leadership,* became a best seller within a few weeks of its release.

Some books on leadership are like Giuliani's, written by successful leaders such as Max DePree, Lee Iacocca, Bill Gates, and Jack Welch, who tell their stories and offer their reflections. Other books provide less personal, more analytical studies on leadership, and still others offer practical help and advice to those who are leaders. The latter — and the fast-growing industry of consultants, coaches, and seminars about leadership that often go with them — usually try to define different styles or types of leaders. For example, Bill Hybels, the pastor of the fast-growing, "seeker-friendly" Willow Creek Church outside Chicago, has written in his book *Courageous Leadership* about ten different leadership styles. It is insightful and helpful. Mentioned earlier were sixteen management and leadership styles based upon one's Myers-Briggs personality typology. Warren Bennis, a popular author on leadership, claimed in his 1985 book, *Leaders: The Strategies for Taking Charge,* to have identified 350 definitions of leadership.

One such approach developed by Brian P. Hall lists seven leadership styles:

Autocratic: All major decisions are made by the person who is in charge, and followed.

Benevolent: The leader is "caringly authoritative," that is, autocratic, but listens well.

Efficient Manager: Clear policies and orderly procedures are emphasized.

Enabler: The focus is on supporting and valuing each person's work.

Charismatic: Inspiration and creativity are provided to the group often in an independent style.

Servant Leadership: Interdependent cooperation in a team with high trust characterize this style.

Prophetic Leadership: Clear value commitments and moral goals propel the leader.*

I've seen this system used as part of a larger research process that tried to identify the values and qualities found in "transformational pastors." Such categories of leadership styles — and there are a plethora to choose from — are always helpful. They push leaders and followers to reflect and analyze dynamics that they are experiencing, but they also carry dangers.

One problem is a rigid adherence to the type or style one has identified as one's own, based upon personality characteristics assumed to be immutable. Of course we all know that we each have personal characteristics that are unlikely to change and provide keys to the strengths of our leadership. Yet gifted leaders also realize that certain behaviors can be modified and adapted in response to one's external environment. One's basic talent, or as the Gallup Organization would say, one's natural "strengths" remain quite constant. But particular skills and styles of action can be learned and

---

*Brian P. Hall, *The Genesis Effect: Personal and Organizational Transformations* (New York: Paulist Press, 1986), 97–133.

developed. *Precisely because change is messy, leaders must be able to change, to shift their own styles as an organization evolves. Leaders cannot remain static in organizations that are adapting and growing.*

Take an organization that knows it needs to focus its mission, cast a vision, and move in new directions. It will need a visionary style of leadership to facilitate that process, a leader who can bring a clear focus to the task but who can also be creative, forward-looking, and directive, able to inspire others to such a journey. For this phase of the journey, their leader should be imaginative and stimulating, always ready to think of new approaches and color outside the lines, capable of expressing and distilling persuasively the issues at the heart of an organization's future and inspiring others to join in a process of dreaming about new possibilities.

But what happens when this organization has successfully moved ahead, embraced a new mission and vision, and now needs to clarify its values and implement these new directions? What is essential at this stage is deep and wide ownership of the mission and vision by the staff, governing bodies, and constituency of the organization. Suddenly the visionary leader, if he or she doesn't change, can get in the way! The leadership style now required is quite different: nurturing, shepherding, encouraging, and clarifying, leadership deeply collegial in style, transparent in its process, and always welcoming the initiative of others. The task of this sort of leadership is to enable the mission and vision to permeate the whole organization.

And then what? Say, through nurturing and clarifying its mission and vision, the organization has internalized its fresh sense of identity, moving toward a new future, and is becoming a cohesive, refocused group. Then leadership needs to change again, providing empowerment to every part and person in the organization, indeed seeking to disperse power as widely as possible, to decentralize authority, and to open new avenues of broad participation to shape each part of the organization's life.

Therefore, leadership is not just vision-casting. It also means building a community around common goals, and empowering and serving others. It all depends on what the organization needs at each stage in its journey, and to be effective, today's leaders need to be able to lead in all *these ways at different points in the life of their organization, and to sense what style of leadership best serves the group at a given time.* Because of the pace of change today, it may well be the case that we don't need different types of leaders as much as we need people who can lead in different types of ways.

To illustrate my point about flexibility in leadership style, a case study can be found in an unlikely but illustrative place — the Lewis and Clark expedition. In the spring of 1804, nearly fifty men began a journey into territory none of them had ever seen nor could barely imagine. One of them, Sergeant Patrick Gass, wrote, "We were to pass through a country possessed of numerous, powerful and warlike nations of savages, of gigantic stature, fierce, treacherous and cruel; and particularly hostile to white men." The expedition was called the Corps of Discovery. Their mission was clear. Two leaders were in charge, Captain Meriwether Lewis and Lieutenant William Clark. Lewis recruited Clark and fully shared leadership and command with him, referring to him as a fellow "captain."

What was their leadership style? How did they enable this incredible, threatening mission to be successfully

accomplished? How did they interact with the members of
the Corps? How did they make decisions? How did they build
community and strengthen morale? Consider three different
examples.

As we might expect, members of the expedition were an
adventurous, unruly group, from a variety of backgrounds:
nine were French-Canadian, and three were sons of Indian
mothers and white fathers. Several of them had already been
part of the army operating in what was then the "frontier"
of the Midwest. Others were simply attracted by the lure of
so challenging a mission.

So in the first months of their mission, Lewis and Clark
had to form this diverse, obstreperous band into a disciplined
group focused on its task and united in its commitment,
which meant establishing clear structures of authority and
accountability. In that first summer, therefore, the journals
of the expedition record that there were no less than five
courts-martial conducted by Lewis and Clark, with offenses
such as getting drunk while on post in the morning, talking back to officers, and falling asleep while on guard. Stern
sentences were given, consisting mostly of lashes on the bare
back, up to one hundred. From this report, we conclude that
Lewis and Clark's leadership style at that time was totally
authoritarian, autocratic, and hierarchical, and at the beginning of the expedition this style was certainly needed.
Though nowadays we would never condone the physical
punishment inflicted with whips and willow branches, I believe we would indeed acknowledge that strict discipline is a
requirement of any group embarking on a perilous mission.

By the fall of that year, the journals no longer record serious incidents of misconduct or court martial. The men in this
Corps of Discovery appear to have been overwhelmed by the

grandeur of the Great Plains, full of wildlife they had never seen and landscapes beyond their imagination. Their mission, however, was already taking far longer than planned, with countless unforeseen obstacles. But through it all they were being molded into a unified ensemble. After camping for the winter at Mandan, North Dakota, Meriwether Lewis wrote: "At this moment, every individual of the party is in good health and excellent spirits; zealously attached to the enterprise, and anxious to proceed; not a whisper of discontent or murmur is to be heard among them; but all in unison act with the most perfect harmony. With such men I have every thing to hope, and but little to fear."

The Corps now headed out through Montana, following the Missouri River toward the Rocky Mountains. The Hidatsas Indians had given some directions, telling them what to expect and how eventually they would arrive at a great waterfall, but in June, the Corps of Discovery came to a fork in the river. One part headed toward the north. It was muddy, like the Missouri they had been following for more than a year. The fork to the left looked clearer. The Corps was facing a decisive moment.

Making the wrong choice could spell disaster for the expedition. They now knew their time was limited by the seasons as well as supplies; they had to make it over the mountains and to the Pacific before winter. For a week, they camped at the fork and explored options in each direction. Together as a unit they discussed and debated the options.

When Lewis returned from exploring the muddy fork to the right and north, he felt convinced it was the wrong one. He and Clark both believed that the river should be getting clearer if it were to lead them eventually over the mountains. But every other person in the expedition disagreed. They were convinced that following the muddy fork, as they had in the past, made the most sense.

In the end, it fell to Lewis and Clark as the leaders to make the final, and lonely, decision. Even though his choice meant a sharp departure from the more habitual pattern, Lewis trusted his intuition, with Clark's support, and they took the south fork to the left. Lewis made this remarkable recording in his journal: "They said very cheerfully that they were ready to follow us any where we thought proper to direct, but that they still thought that the other was the (main) river and that they were afraid the South fork would soon terminate in the mountains and leave us a great distance from the Columbia."

As is clear here, by this time concerns about "talking back to officers" no longer were an issue of discipline. Instead, a shared sense of allegiance and trust had developed among them all. Opinions were invited, perspectives were shared, and yet the recognized leaders made the final decision, having so earned the trust of the company that its members both felt able to express their differing views but also give their full support as a united body once the decision was made. Within a few days, Lewis heard the distant sound of waterfalls. He and Clark had made the right choice.

When they reached their destination at the mouth of the Columbia River, the Corps faced another critical decision. Where would they make camp for the winter? Right by the ocean, more exposed to treacherous weather but with the chance that they might spot a ship? Or at a more protected site inland, along the Columbia? In this case, after discussion and exploration, Lewis and Clark submitted the decision to a democratic vote of the Corps. The trust and cohesion of the group meant that in this case the leaders put the highest value on empowering each member and giving over their authority in this decision to the will of the whole group. Even the one black slave who was part of the Corps was given a vote. The majority decided to make camp by the ocean and built what became Fort Clatsop.

Leadership is, of course, essential for a group to be productive and accomplish its mission. But as Lewis and Clark illustrate for us, leaders are most effective when they have the wisdom and security to adapt their style of leadership to the dynamics of their organization and the requirements of their mission over time. The flexibility of Lewis and Clark as leaders was in large part why their expedition was able to accomplish its incredible mission of discovery.

19

Personality Types and Change

My wife, Karin, is an accomplished gardener and enjoys her pastime with a passion. Over the past nine years, the yard around our home has been completely transformed, and often I've joined in helping with various tasks. The grass of our front lawn ends at the sidewalk by the street like most of the lawns around us. Our street can get busy at times, as it serves as the main route up the hill to our local high school, but overall, our home is in a pleasant setting, with a yard and gardens that stretch back behind the house to a wooded area. In the summer we love to spend time out back on our deck away from the sometimes noisy street.

One Saturday morning I joined Karin in our front yard. "You know, I've been imagining how we could change this front yard," she began. "We need something between the street and the yard, maybe like a berm, but something that sets the whole yard off and separates it from the street. It would give us more protection from the traffic and would connect the planting we've done by our driveway across to our neighbor's driveway."

I had no idea what she was talking about, so I just stood there and stared, trying to visualize what she saw so clearly in her mind. But all I could see was a perfectly fine front yard ending nicely at the sidewalk and street. However, I've learned to trust her instincts and vision, and so I didn't just dismiss what she was saying out of hand. Finally, still with considerable skepticism, I said, "Well, what would you like me to do?"

That was just what she was waiting for. "We've got to kill all the grass within about three feet of the sidewalk, but not in a straight line, in kind of an arch, so it can connect with the bed on the right of the drive, and then curl back down until it reaches the raised bed by the drive next door. You can cut it real short, get old newspapers, lay them out, soak them, and then we'll need to cover it all with wood chips."

In the end, mutual trust is the "coin of the realm" in organizations embarked on the journey of change.

By now, I was sorry I had asked, for a whole new set of questions started racing through my mind. Was she serious? Did she know what this would take? Think of how much newspaper would actually be required. And then the wood chips — where would we get those? How much would this cost? Beyond all of these details, did she have any idea of how much time this would take? Or the wear and tear on my back? I was still trying to get a clear picture of what this would look like when it was done, and why it would be an improvement, as I started the lawnmower.

Today our front yard is marked off by a crescent shaped border filled with rose bushes, evergreens, and flowering shrubs. It visually and literally connects gardens on either side of our yard and, moreover, provides a pleasant division between the edge of the front sidewalk and the yard. In fact, it looks like it had been designed that way from the start because it simply makes so much aesthetic sense. That is what Karin saw, the vision in her mind's eye, when we stood there together that Saturday morning.

From this experience with my wife, I understand a little better how my staff often responds to me. I may have talked incessantly about the vision for the future of the Reformed Church in America, painted it with moving word pictures, and spelled out what it will take to get there. And yet some staff responded to me as I did to Karin. They couldn't see the vision. They wondered what difference it would make. They questioned whether I and others had a workable plan and had carefully counted the costs, and they worried about what it would cost them.

As mentioned earlier, each year we take most of a week in a retreat setting for what we call "Staff Reflection Days." The executive staff of the denomination who work out of offices in different geographical locations gather together for a time of community building to address issues of importance in our life together. When we were in the early stages of implementing our Statement of Mission and Vision, we asked a management consultant who is a member of one of our congregations, Cecil Williams, and another gifted consultant and author, Nancy J. Barger, to help us deal with how we were responding to organizational change.

With Linda K. Kirby, Barger has written *The Challenge of Change in Organizations: Helping Employees Thrive in the New Frontier,* a book that examines how people deal with organizational change differently, according to our Myers-Briggs personality type. This was the approach used by these

consultants with our staff. The book also employs the metaphor of a wagon train traveling from St. Louis to Oregon
as a way of picturing an organization on a journey, heading
for a new destination, and this picture worked well for our
situation. To prepare for the retreat, therefore, all the staff
had taken the Myers-Briggs type indicator. Since sixteen different types are possible, these can be pictured in a grid with
sixteen squares, four to a side. The names of all the staff
were placed in this grid in their appropriate box.

The result was revealing. Because several key staff leaders
were "INTJs," that is to say, Introvert, Intuitive, Thinking,
Judging, it made complete sense that other staff, in a process
of change, yearned for more information to be communi-
cated from these introverted leaders. It also made sense that
"Sensates" on our staff—people who value concrete data—
were impatient with visionary pictures and nervous about
what these changes would cost and how their daily work
would be affected.

Each personality type responds uniquely, with potential
strengths and weaknesses, to the process of organizational
change. Extroverted, intuitive, thinking types, for instance,
can be enthusiastic, clear, and innovative, but if they are
stressed, or disregarded, they can become almost frantic,
constantly oversimplifying situations, and criticizing others.
Introverted, sensing, feeling types can be empathetic, sensitive, and reflective in the process of change, but when
ignored or discounted, they can become hypersensitive,
emotional "rescuers," paralyzed from taking action. Such
positive and negative tendencies can be elaborated for each
personality type over the whole grid of sixteen possible types.

In the end, mutual trust is the "coin of the realm" in
organizations embarked on the journey of change. As we

talked together during that staff retreat, we realized our experience could be compared to a wagon train headed for the Oregon Trail. We had a vision of where we were going, and that motivated us, but we had little idea of what we might encounter along the way. To get there successfully, each person would have a role to play, but we all would need to have mutual trust in one another. If people feel that their particular gifts and personalities are valued and can contribute something that is needed, they are likely to offer what they can to the process of organizational change. They may not have all their questions answered or all their anxieties relaxed. But if enough mutual trust is created through respect for each person's personality type, they will be able to say as I did to my wife, "Where would you like me to start?"

20

The Challenge of Organizational Growth

Organizations are living organisms and go through stages of development and growth. But how are new organizations born? Usually a person, who becomes the leader, is gripped with a strong sense of discontinuity between what is and what could be, and has a passionate sense of how certain things should be different from the present. Such individuals are able to imagine an alternative future, and that is foundational to bringing a new organization into being. In business, an entrepreneur is convinced that a new product or service will find a market. In the religious world, a new church development pastor, or "church planter," envisions a new, vibrant congregation meeting the needs of people who presently have no church home. The social activist whose conscience is tormented by a glaring injustice that is morally indefensible moves forward with passion to form an advocacy or social service initiative. Often described as "charismatic," meaning they are gifted with the capacity to inspire others, founders are obsessed with a drive to change some dimension of social, political, economic, or religious reality, and thus conceive and give birth to new organizations.

Consider an example distant from our modern context: St. Francis of Assisi. Born into a life of wealth and comfort in Italy, he had an intense encounter with God that changed his life and endowed him with a startling vision of an alternative reality. Deeply grieved by the plight of the poor amid the affluent, he sold all he had and undertook a life of simple poverty, passionately believing that the church of his time had lost its way and needed to reform itself to follow more faithfully the teachings and example of its founder, Jesus Christ.

Francis's actions were stunning, and gradually he began to attract a following as others saw in his witness a way of faith and life that they wanted to share. In time, what had been his individual vision began to become a movement, and eventually a religious order of the Roman Catholic Church. Today thousands of Franciscans both lay and ordained live by the model of Christian faithfulness that he inspired.

When organizations begin, such charismatic, visionary leaders attract followers, and during this initial stage, there is near-complete faith in and loyalty to this leader, which means that at this point such organizations generally operate with great inner cohesion and generally hierarchical ways of making decisions. The founding leader is in control, and there is little deviation from what he or she desires. Even when there may be different rhetoric and structures about authority and decision-making, in practical terms such emerging organizations are almost wholly governed by their leader.

In some ways, this dynamic is a natural one, especially when the organization is moving against the status quo, motivated by a sharp, alternative vision of what can be. By definition, the group's purpose or mission is in deep discontinuity with surrounding society or culture, which is a source of significant external stress and tension. If it is also beset internally with conflict and sharp disagreement, therefore, an organization usually cannot succeed in this founding phase without the cohesion and solidarity brought to it by the founder.

However, when an organization has successfully established itself, a new phase of life begins. As the followers gain in their own self-confidence, they also begin to see that their founding leader has clay feet and that not every decision or judgment made by the leader is right. Members begin to ask questions, offer suggestions, and often make criticisms both of the leader and the way the organization functions. This change in relationship between the leader and members marks a defining passage in the life of an organization and tests the capacity of its founding leader. One of two courses is possible. First, the leader may determine that the most pressing need is for the vision of the organization to be internalized far more deeply by its membership; in other words, a clear transition needs to be made from following the *leader* to following the *vision*.

In this case, as the membership (or staff, or congregation, or employees) truly claim the vision as their own, other things will change. The original vision itself may be modified, and that can be a healthy step. Recasting and clarifying the founding vision, within certain parameters, needs to be at least a possibility if the vision is to be genuinely reflected in the whole of the organization, and not just in its leader. Further, patterns of decision-making and authority will be altered. As the vision is more broadly internalized by members of the whole organization, power and control need to be decentralized so that members have real responsibility for ensuring that the core mission of the organization is carried out. Here a governing board or council often takes on a more decisive role, truly becoming the "trustees" of the founder's vision, having the authority to take steps to see that this vision can be sustained in ways that are not totally dependent upon the founding leader.

When a new church is begun, for instance, it almost always faces a crisis within the first five to seven years of its life that revolves around the need for the founding pastor to change his or her role with the congregation.

Nevertheless, the role of the leader remains vital. He or she continues to project and articulate the original vision and in most cases remains the public spokesperson and symbol of the organization's purpose, inspiring, empowering, encouraging, advising, and thanking those who now carry the responsibility for its implementation. As long as this founding leader is present, he or she continues to look at the far horizon and dream of where the organization's vision could still take them.

But as an organization founded on a charismatic leader's vision grows, another less positive set of developments may occur. The original leader may continue to insist on unquestioned loyalty, meeting criticism with defensiveness and casting judgments on those who raise questions, believing that the membership or staff of the organization are not yet ready to share greater responsibility. In the leader's view, power needs to be carefully controlled and protected, for, if not, the leader fears that the vision will be diluted or lost. In this alternative scenario, the founding leader responds with continued demands for trust from follower, but evinces little willingness to trust them in return. The organization may be able to continue — primarily because its vision is true and powerful — but many key and creative persons will simply leave, and those who remain are likely to be dependent personalities. Thus, the leader's fear that others in the organization are not ready to share central responsibility becomes a self-fulfilling prophecy. I've seen this happen; it's tragic, and sometimes it gets ugly. In such cases, the organization is usually not able to continue once the founding leader is gone from the scene. **Sometimes organizational death comes even more quickly as the crisis created by such an organization's initial success leads to enormous and fatal internal conflicts that sabotage and undo its potential.**

These stages in the initial development of organizations are very predictable. I've observed them occurring within new churches, in radical Christian communities, in non-profit organizations, in major social justice advocacy groups, and in Christian ministries with multimillion-dollar budgets. When a new church is begun, for instance, it almost always faces a crisis within the first five to seven years of its life that revolves around the need for the founding pastor to change his or her role with the congregation. Some can do so, and others have the wisdom to welcome new leadership and move on, often to start another new congregation. In all these situations, however, the self-understanding of the leader is of paramount importance. If the leader understands these dynamics, transitions through these phases can occur smoothly, and the focus remains on living out the founding vision. But this requires psychological maturity and healthy spiritual detachment on the part of the leader. Further, understanding and addressing the developmental phases of an organization should be a focus of its governing board. When organizations make a healthy transition from being founded to being sustained, it usually comes from nurturing a creative, honest partnership between its founding leader and its key members or governing board.

21

The Arduous Journey of Transformation

While the stresses and challenges facing newly formed organizations are unique, established organizations face the more common but arduous task of discovering paths for their revitalization and renewal. If organizations are organisms that go through stages of development and growth, then they also can be subject to atrophy, decay, and death. Often, even organizations with an inspiring history and unique purpose can find themselves struggling between possibilities of growth and revitalization, and threats of deterioration and institutional death.

For six years I served on the staff of the World Council of Churches as director of Church and Society and in other capacities, and for the past decade I have been a member of its governing board. Through these years I participated in WCC's long and difficult journey of organizational transformation, which often felt like a struggle between vitality and decay, and remains an unfinished task. Located in Geneva, Switzerland, where an international staff carries out its various programs, the WCC links together 342 Christian denominations, or "communions," from all parts and cultures of the world to build unity and strengthen a common Christian witness and action in the world. In 1989 its governing board, called the Central Committee, initiated a major process to identify what was termed the "Common Understanding and Vision of the World Council of Churches." At that point many people inside and outside the organization were sensing that the WCC's style of holding consultations, producing educational resources, and sending out reports often served particular interest groups and concerns but was no longer widely engaging the WCC's member churches in fresh ecumenical commitments. To many of its member denominations and communions around the world, the WCC was perceived as an international bureaucracy in Geneva, doing some useful tasks like other nongovernmental organizations, but not effective in calling its member churches themselves into ecumenical engagement with each other and in the world.

The Common Understanding and Vision process, as it evolved, attempted to transform how the WCC's member churches related to one another and internalized the ecumenical calling of the WCC as their own. All this took an extraordinary amount of time — nearly eight years — due in part to the complexity of the organization and the need for wide participation.

The WCC general secretary at the time, Dr. Konrad Raiser, focused his attention, careful analysis, and creative energy around this Common Understanding and Vision process, with the belief that this had the best hope of revitalizing the ecumenical commitment of the WCC's member churches and refocusing the style and future direction of the WCC's work as it prepared to celebrate its fiftieth anniversary. Governing Board meetings, study papers, and consultations around the world, attempting to draw in voices from all its constituencies, were engaged in this process. Various drafting teams worked hard on what became a long and comprehensive text, but while this lengthy process created hope and enthusiasm in some circles, it generated anxiety in others.

As the process stretched on, the WCC's staff became destabilized. Already besieged by financial pressures, the staff now found themselves observing a process largely out of their control, one that could dramatically alter the institution to which they had given their vocational lives. I vividly remember one highly respected senior staff member, after a particularly lively and creative Central Committee discussion on the draft document, confiding to me in total consternation, "Does anyone have any idea where all this is really going?"

Morale at the WCC plummeted, and a few very gifted staff members decided to leave. Others who stayed directed private, stinging criticisms toward the general secretary, and some others simply tried to focus on their own narrow areas of concern while skeptically dismissing the whole process. Still other colleagues pleaded for clarity, closure, and action, and those concerned about finances pressed to link the potential implications of the process to specific budgets and resources, which all remained very unclear. And if all this wasn't enough, special centers of programmatic work in the WCC began overtly worrying that the directions of this emerging common vision might leave them out or marginalize their voice and power. Lobbying campaigns were launched, and mutual trust was becoming fragile. During this time it often seemed as though the organization was in a downward spiral that threatened its ongoing viability and life.

Yet the WCC persisted in the process as Dr. Raiser and other key players kept setting forth the challenge of the council's Common Understanding and Vision, inviting everyone into the dialogue. At the same time, a parallel process of internal staff reorganization was initiated along with the engagement of a consultant to help the staff work on issues of the organizational culture.

In September 1997 the Central Committee of the WCC approved the final text of its Common Understanding and Vision, and the next year this was affirmed at the WCC's Eighth Assembly — a gathering of delegates from every member church that takes place every seven years. Constitutional changes that resulted were approved as well, and we held a fiftieth-year celebration of recommitment.

But since that time, implementation of the Common Understanding and Vision has been arduous. As mentioned earlier, the Orthodox churches, longtime members of the Council, felt increasingly estranged and marginalized from the WCC's agenda, working style, and ethos. A fifty-member Special Commission, half from Orthodox churches and half from other WCC members, worked for three years until eventually finding common ground for moving forward. For some within the WCC this process with the Orthodox churches demonstrated the deeper way of relating between member churches made possible by the Council's Common Understanding and Vision.

All the same, financial pressures on the organization steadily grew worse in this period, putting the overall commitment of member churches to the WCC to a real test. Broader financial trends and poor management decisions

depleted WCC's financial reserves, and as pressures for solutions to the Council's ongoing sustainability grew stronger,
a focus on its common vision seemed to fade. Against this
background, the WCC launched a search for a new general
secretary as the term of Dr. Raiser came to a close. Dr. Sam
Kobia was eventually selected, the WCC's first general secretary from Africa, and as he began his service in January
2004, the WCC showed signs of regaining some financial sta-
bility due in part to major staff reductions. Dr. Kobia faces
the challenge of revitalizing the ecumenical imagination that
is at the heart of the WCC's strength and engaging the diverse parts of the global Christian community in this calling.
Clearly, our journey of organizational transformation at the
WCC still has a long way to go, and much will depend upon
leadership that can empower the underlying spiritual vision
that sustains the ecumenical movement.

At Harvard University, Ronald A. Heifetz directs the
John F. Kennedy School of Government's Center for Public
Leadership, and his book *Leadership without Easy Answers* has
been widely acclaimed. More recently he co-authored with
Marty Linsky *Leadership on the Line,* and one of its helpful insights is the distinction between what are called "technical"
challenges in an organization and "adaptive" challenges.

Technical problems are those that have a clear definition
and an available solution and implementation, e.g., reduce a
budget by 25 percent. To do so may not be easy or painless,
but it is clear and possible and can be accomplished by those
with authority. Adaptive challenges, on the other hand, do
not have solutions that are immediately apparent. They require experimentation and learning and normally involve
changes in behavior, values, and attitudes of those in the
organization.

Heifetz argues that the most frequent cause of leadership failure is that adaptive challenges are treated like technical problems, a mistake commonly made in times of stress. In *Leadership on the Line* with Marty Linsky, they say, "In the face of adaptive pressures, people don't want questions, they want answers. They don't want to be told they will have to sustain losses; rather they want to know how you're going to protect them from the pains of change.... In mobilizing adaptive work, you have to engage people in adjusting their unrealistic expectations, rather than satisfy them as if the situation is amenable primarily to a technical remedy.... This takes an extraordinary level of presence, time, and artful communication."

Organizations in situations like the World Council of Churches face concrete technical problems, to be sure, such as how to build a sustainable budget, but in reality the deepest issue is what Heifetz calls an adaptive challenge, how to reshape the culture and ethos of an organization to express its common vision. The answers to such a challenge require experimentation and discernment; they come through identifying deeper underlying questions that need to be faced, even when their answers are not immediately apparent. The ways forward are discovered together and embraced, rather than imposed, and in the process the leader serves as a guide to the community's journey of transformation. Those able to guide such journeys successfully can be called transformational leaders.

Charisma alone in a leader isn't enough, for inspiring people is not the same as leading them. Many charismatic, gifted leaders fail, and the institutions they serve are crippled when they become incapable of channeling the power of their vision into organization transformation. At the same time, other leaders fail because they value organizational co-herence above all else. They see their task as holding the organization together rather than moving the organization forward. While they may have significant skills in conflict management and know how to gain approval from diverse factions in the organization, they are often unable to institute changes essential for future growth. In their focus on maintenance rather than mission, they also are unable to be transformational leaders.

But what, exactly, then is meant by "transformational leadership"? Writing in 1978 in his now classic book titled simply *Leadership*, James MacGregor Burns, perhaps the most influential thinker and writer on leadership in recent times, first defined "transformational leadership" and contrasted this with what he termed "transactional leadership." For Burns, "transactional leadership" occurs when a leader enables a group to achieve some end it desires and is provided in return with support or some other service. Simply put, it is a style of leadership that operates on a "You scratch my back, and I'll scratch yours" basis. Such leadership rests on seeing that the self-interest of various individuals and groups, as well as the leader, is met through various trade-offs and exchanges, hence the term "transactional leadership."

Mayor Richard Daley (Sr.), who ruled Chicago in the 1960s and 1970s, provides a classic political example of such leadership. His well-developed political "machine" met the needs of various groups and constituents. Certain neighborhoods got good streetlights, particular construction companies got contracts, and people got political patronage jobs in exchange for loyalty and service to Daley's political apparatus. Indeed, "transactional leadership" guides much of politics even if it is not as brutish and blatant as the political machine of Mayor Daley. The astonishing growth of money as a central factor in political campaigns over the past couple of decades has strongly reinforced this "transactional" style of political leadership. Rightly or wrongly, individuals and groups who contribute enormous sums to candidates expect quid pro quo, and candidates promise to meet specific needs and desires of such supporters in tacit exchange for money received.

Burns contrasts transactional leadership with transformational leadership. In the latter, the motives of the leader and the followers go beyond mutual self-interest. Rather, broader purposes, rooted in particular moral and ethical values, guide their actions so that the relationship between leader and followers functions differently, for they have been united together out of a set of growing shared convictions. A transformational leader is able to direct the loyalty of those in an organization or constituency beyond their immediate self-interest to a far greater purpose and vision that enlists their heartfelt commitment.

Of course, in proposing this paradigm for analyzing types of leadership, Burns and others after him understand that transactional and transformational styles are actually two ends of a continuum rather than a strict either/or. Effective transformational leaders, especially in politics, often build from a transactional base and are able to move followers or constituents from seeing that their self-interest is served to joining together in the mutual service of moral goals that transcend their own immediate needs and desires.

During the time when I served as a staff assistant to Senator Mark O. Hatfield, I watched the senator function between these two ends of this continuum and take his followers with him. As one of the earliest opponents of the

Vietnam War, while he was still governor of Oregon Hatfield cast the sole vote against Lyndon Johnson's Vietnam policies at the 1966 National Governors Conference. Once elected to the U.S. Senate, he emerged as one of the major political leaders of antiwar sentiment in the nation, particularly in the wake of the U.S. invasion of Cambodia and the Kent State shooting in 1970. Yet by 1972 his political base in Oregon was weakening, and polls showed he was in danger of losing his Senate seat in the election of that year. Though millions around the country were deeply influenced by the transformational leadership he had exercised around Vietnam, his contribution to the nation on that issue didn't translate into an electoral majority in his own home state; throughout the nation at that time, opposition to the Vietnam War was forceful and growing, but still politically a minority opinion.

Hatfield responded by convincing the Oregon electorate that he could serve the needs of the state effectively and well, essentially adopting a "transactional" strategy. His influence on the Senate Appropriations Committee, he argued, could win funding for needed projects to develop Oregon's harbors, secure its power supply, sustain its forestry industry, and protect its environment. His opposition to the war never diminished, but he used his transactional leadership to win reelection so as to continue his transformational leadership on Vietnam.

James MacGregor Burns details many specific characteristics and ways for exercising such leadership, and history provides many vivid examples — Gandhi, Lech Walesa, Nelson Mandela, and Pope John XXIII. In all these leaders, their vision for change, rooted in moral and ethical concerns, was translated effectively into a movement that dramatically altered political or ecclesiastical structures and so affected the course of world history.

But transformational leadership need not be grand. The school board president, the pastor, priest, or rabbi, the director of a homeless shelter, and the head of a local chapter of the Sierra Club can exercise it. Certain ingredients always seem to be present. Warren Bennis, in *Strategies for Taking Charge* written with Burt Nanus, identifies these as: having vision, being able to interpret meaning, gaining trust of followers, and possessing self-confidence. I would add courage, openness to continual learning, and the ability to crystallize key insights and truths from complex information.

Some transformational leaders also exercise enormous influence for change even when they are not in formal positions of political or institutional authority. Martin Luther King Jr. is perhaps the clearest example of such leadership from recent American history. Within the Catholic Church, both Dorothy Day and Thomas Merton demonstrated leadership while not possessing or seeking positions of formal religious authority. And we could regard former President Jimmy Carter, winner of the 2002 Nobel Peace Prize, as one who has exercised greater transformational leadership over the years since his presidency than when he actually held the world's most powerful political position.

You know when you are in the presence of transformational leaders. It's not just that they are charismatic. Articulating a compelling vision, they also unearth deep meaning and make sense out of a complex and confusing reality. Further, they demonstrate that they can be trusted and you feel invited by them. In those times of crisis when organizations seem to hang in the balance between creativity and growth or deterioration and death, transformational leaders have a way of galvanizing those in the organization around developments that lead to life and vitality. These are the leaders capable of creating and renewing institutions and even, at times, transforming history.

22

Forming Teams That Perform

Transformational leaders who revitalize organizations never can do so alone. They become skilled in creating an organizational culture that fosters teams that work, for that's how the tasks of orienting an organization around a vision and focusing on its mission are best actually implemented. Few would argue, and the rhetoric about teams is plentiful in most organizations and corporations today, but the reality is often different. A definition of what constitutes a team is frequently not clear, and so groups given the label of "team" do not function like one, and power and effectiveness essential to teams is withheld from the organization as a whole.

Some years ago, not long after beginning as general secretary, I faced an organizational dilemma within the staff of the Reformed Church in America. Many were critical of the administrative groups and internal structure that governed our life; morale seemed low, and communication was poor. We gathered a representative group on retreat, listened to each other, and then decided to scrap the existing staff cabinet, which many felt was too inaccessible, replacing it with three new more inclusive groups: the Leadership Advisory Team, the Management and Administration Team, and the Program and Coordination Team.

This bit of reorganization was an improvement and did help to solve the problems we had faced. Only later did I realize that while these groups performed important functions, none of them really was a team according to the truest definition of that term. Simply calling a group a team doesn't make it so.

Jon R. Katzenbach has spent years analyzing what constitutes a team and how teams function within organizations. More than ten years ago, in 1993, he co-authored, with Douglas K. Smith, *The Wisdom of Teams: Creating the High-Performance Organization* published by the Harvard Business School Press. Five years later he wrote *Teams at the Top*. Katzenbach and Smith argue that while "teamwork" means an important set of values needed in organizations, the definition of what constitutes a team is much more precise: "A team is a small number of people with complementary skills who are committed to a common purpose, set of performance goals, and approach for which they hold themselves mutually accountable" (*Teams at the Top*, 217).

In this sense, teams are a group set aside for a specific purpose. That purpose might be to establish clear admission standards for a college, design a new communications strategy for a hundred thousand members of an environmental advocacy group, or figure out how to invite unchurched members of a community to visit a congregation. Sometimes a broader directive that calls a team into being, such as significantly increasing the membership and participation of young people in an established organization, will lead to specific goals adopted by that team, such as launching an interactive online newsletter.

Teams by this definition have clear performance objectives. They know when they have accomplished their purpose. Moreover, the specificity of their goals and objectives helps the team members to internalize their authority and to work as equals. Titles and positions in the overall organization matter less than how each person contributes to accomplishing the specific objective of the team. For this reason teams need to be given a clear mandate and the power to achieve it — to recommend something, solve a problem, or operate a critical organizational function. Once given that power, team members can hold one another accountable for achieving their goal.

When teams in this sense come together, they form their own group dynamic. Of those who have studied this dynamic, Bruce Tuckman, in 1965, identified four stages in a team's development: forming, storming, norming, and performing. In the "forming" phase, teams become clear about their purpose or mission, create a vision of what its success might look like, understand the context in which the team will operate, agree on its procedures, and share one another's strengths, experience, and expectations. Teams usually have a team leader, sometimes appointed or chosen by the team itself. In this first phase of "forming," the group depends on the leader to get them going.

The "storming" phase can be the most volatile, for this is when the team must agree on strategies, create a work plan, decide on a method of leadership and mutual accountability, and develop its working style. If conflict is to occur within a team, it usually comes at this point. The diversity of operating styles, personal temperaments, and approaches to the team's purpose need to be reconciled, and it may be a stormy process. The temptation is often to "sweep this under the rug," but doing so simply means that problems are postponed to a time when they will ultimately inflict damage on the team's performance.

The "norming" phase comes as progress toward the goal begins to be made. The task then is to maintain focus so the team stays on track. It begins to settle into a comfortable style, and the level of trust increases, which leads to the "performing" phase, as a team begins to achieve its objective and meet specific goals. The question at this point becomes how much further the team can go, and how it can help to integrate its discoveries into the wider life of the organization. The team celebrates its successes but also seeks to learn from its failures along the way. By the time the team reaches its last phase, leadership within such a team becomes widely shared, so naturally the team leader functions far differently than he or she did at the start, since the task now is empowering and affirming team members and encouraging future progress. Depending on its purpose, a team may come to an end when its objective is achieved, or it may be given ongoing responsibilities for implementation.

My experience is that such teams will develop like microcosms of the larger organization, reflecting the progression experienced by most groups that commit themselves to the journey of change. The analogy shared earlier about changing styles of leadership in the Lewis and Clark expedition is echoed in this portrayal of stages in the life of a team.

How might such wisdom apply to the church? First, it seems that this secular definition of teams and their stages mirrors the calling of believers into specific groups or bands of disciples. Jesus carried out his mission through forming a team, and the gospels testify that this was often a stormy process. As the New Testament pictures the development of the early church, the model is that each person functions out of the particular "gift" he or she has, which must be utilized within a deeply interdependent group. First Corinthians 12, for instance, paints a graphic picture of each person serving as a member of a body where literally one part cannot function outside of its relationship to the whole. That's the opposite of achievement based on individualistic accomplishment and stresses the mutual accountability of the members to one another.

Models of how congregations are governed in practice cover a continuum from strict hierarchy to almost pure democracy. But the core of biblical insight, I would argue, stresses collegial models that guide and govern the life of the local church. In traditions rooted in the Protestant Reformation, for instance, elders, deacons, and the pastor form a consistory to nurture and direct the congregation; when functioning well, it's like a true team. The problem in most congregations, however, is that such groups place most of their focus on administrative matters and lose sight of a guiding vision for their ministry. Congregations engaged in the process of revitalization, however, usually see the function of their consistory or governing body change and become much more like a team. Further, such congregations often end up dissolving existing committees and instead call together teams based on those with passion and gifts for functions such as worship, outreach, discipleship, and mission. These teams function much more dynamically, often reflecting the qualities of teams that function well in secular organizations guided by transformational leadership.

Typically, teams don't replace a whole organizational structure. Rather, they supplement and strengthen it. So whether in a church or a secular institution, when should a team be formed? Katzenbach and Smith provide a good answer:

"A team opportunity exists anywhere hierarchy or organizational boundaries inhibit the skills and perspectives needed for optimal results."

Organizations need clear goals and objectives, derived from their vision and mission, to provide the context in which teams can effectively function. Discerning, self-assured leaders will learn to empower and trust such teams. They will be guided by this simple maxim: "None of us is as good as all of us." Or, as in the African proverb shared by Dr. Sam Kobia when he was elected the new general secretary of the World Council of Churches, "If you want to go fast, walk alone. If you want to go far, walk together."

23

Telling Our Stories

Transformational leaders learn the power of stories and utilize them to guide, shape, and inspire an organization. Dr. David Roe, president of Central College in Pella, Iowa, gives an annual "State of the College" address and an update at the start of each semester. When visiting the campus for a lecture, I heard Dr. Roe's report, which includes stories from what he calls his "Gee Whiz" file. Through the year, Dr. Roe asks faculty and staff simply to send him stories of students and graduates that demonstrate concrete ways that the values and goals of the college are being lived out. Then he shares several of these with the whole college community. It's a simple but effective technique for people to see through these examples, and not just through rhetoric, how and where the college is succeeding in its mission.

Effective preachers also know that they can best communicate the truth of a scriptural passage by telling a story that illustrates its point, because a story is what people remember. Jesus taught that way as well. The parables of the prodigal son, the good Samaritan, the good shepherd, and so many more all translate enduring truths into specific, human situations, and they continue to communicate with power after two thousand years.

Effective leaders also come to understand the power of sharing their own personal stories with others, in appropriate ways, for people desire to know the experiences that molded a leader's character and motivate his or her commitments. It's common for people to think of their own life's journey as an unfolding story. When individuals take the time to reflect on their life, they understand the successive episodes and chapters they have lived and that have shaped them into the distinct person they presently are.

It's a gift to be able to share one's story with another, and unfortunately that gift is not often given to us. Our culture is geared to immediate, pressing events, to the "breaking news" of both our society and our personal lives, so perspective on the longer story of our life's journey can be hard to come by. It's difficult to acknowledge how the real story of our life is not just the outward, chronological sequence of birth, childhood, schooling, career, marriage, children, job changes, retirement, and so on, but also our inward journey toward the discovery of our truest self. Those of religious faith understand that this is only possible through our on-going encounter with God. That provides the most exciting, and often most tumultuous narrative in anyone's life. For that reason, we need to tell these stories. They help us to develop the "long picture" of who we are. Sometimes in the very telling of the past we find new freedom and clarity in the present.

When I became a member of Church of the Saviour in Washington, D.C., the last step in the process was to write a "spiritual autobiography" and share this with the church council. No superficial account of pious moments, my task was to present a thorough telling of my pilgrimage as I experienced both God's absence and presence in my life. As a young adult, this was the first occasion when I had ever taken the time to carefully chart the course of my inward journey. Thirty years later, the memory of sitting and sharing my story with the church council remains strong, a deeply affirming and liberating experience for me. But such opportunities to tell our stories are rare, and ironically, pastors — the leaders of congregations who enable the narrative of Christian faith to intersect the stories of those in the church community — often have little or no opportunity to share their own personal stories. Frequently today pastors become depleted, feeling torn in too many directions, overwhelmed by expectations and uncertain of their future calling, demands that render it particularly urgent for them to find a safe space to share deeply and vulnerably the story of their journey with God.

Craig Dykstra, vice president of religion for the Lilly Endowment, has helped guide the stewardship of millions of dollars to study and support measures that sustain pastors in the excellence of their service. From all this wealth of experience, Dykstra concludes that two factors, above all, are most important in enabling pastors to serve long and well. The first he calls "pastoral imagination," by which he means the ability to see beyond the surface of situations and persons with a depth of insight and understanding. The second is the creation of small groups where pastors can safely tell their stories and share their lives. Duke Divinity School did research that verified this finding. They asked pastors who had clearly succeeded in their ministry what had sustained them, and the most frequent response was friendship. They then asked pastors whose service in ministry was disappointing what was the most destructive factor in their experience, and the most frequent response was isolation.

In our denomination, a team of leaders has been facilitating networks of small groups for pastors to enable them to share their stories. In fact, our staff has become convinced that the key to revitalizing the life of congregations that seem to be stagnating or losing their vitality is to begin by providing such opportunities to pastors for reflection on their own stories. About 250 pastors have become involved in such network groups, and they all are based on covenantal accountability, collegial support, and transformational learning. Within a small, committed group of pastors they may well spend a year in this kind of sharing with one another, and then, as they become clear about God's call in their present and future ministry, other key members of their congregation are invited into a similar process.

Telling one's story is not easy. First, a high degree of safety and trust needs to be established within such a group as part of its covenant from the start, and members may take some time to test the integrity of this commitment. In such testing, bonds begin to be built, however, that can bear the weight of revealing the travail and longing of each person's soul.

Certain tools can also help, for instance, charting out one's spiritual story visually using a timeline. On the top of a very wide sheet of paper, one makes a long line representing the chronology of one's life, and enters key times — birth, baptism, high school graduation, vocational chapters, etc. Then, on a parallel line below, one notes the "sacred places" in one's spiritual journey: a summer camp, a church, a college dorm room, or a vacation cabin — those physical spaces where one had experiences of a formative encounter with God. Next, on a third parallel line below, one records the names of the "sacred people" in his or her life, and when they intersected one's journey. We all learn faith from others. Usually there are two or three particular individuals in our life who serve as mentors and mediators of our religious experience, who came to us at specific points and shaped, molded, intervened, and opened us to a fresh chapter of our story. Finally, on a fourth parallel line below, one lists those specific "sacred events" that indelibly have marked one's spiritual journey — a baptism, a conversion experience, a mystical encounter with the holy, a sermon, a book read, a pastoral conversation — moments that became pivotal events shaping one's spiritual development. When completed, the person has a visual picture that reveals his or her spiritual story and enables it to be told and absorbed. It may also provide striking clarity for the direction that this story is unfolding and even suggest the next steps God is beckoning one to take.

Keeping a journal of this journey is another tool that can help one see the long picture, and I've done so intermittently for the past thirty years as a kind of spiritual therapy, touching deep places within me psychologically and emotionally. Shortly after I first began this practice, I spent one month living with monks at a Trappist Monastery near Berryville, Virginia. I was engaged to be married in a few months, and my future wife, Karin, was teaching in Japan. During those weeks an intense combination of dreams, prayers, reflections, and extensive writing in my journal constituted in retrospect something like a psychoanalytic experience as I encountered depths of insight into myself and experienced deep levels of inner healing. Often I've reflected that this time was the best possible preparation for our marriage.

More recently, I faced another pivotal life decision when I was nominated to be one of the candidates for general secretary of the World Council of Churches. Over the course of

some months, while on a sabbatical, I returned to my journals, reflecting on my past history and then listening and
writing reflections on what I was sensing as I took a time
of retreat for this purpose at St. Benedict's Monastery in
Snowmass, Colorado. The abbot there, Father Joseph, asked
me a simple question: "What particular shape do you think
Christ is taking in your life at this particular point in your
journey?" In time, an answer came with inner clarity and
peace that I should withdraw my name from the WCC's
process and continue my present service. A few weeks later
I was at lunch with friends in Manhattan and related this
story. One replied with words that captured so well my experience, "The hardest thing we have to do in life is to try to
listen to God. And the problem is, God speaks in whispers,
and doesn't always complete his sentences."

When we open our hearts to listen intently for God's call,
we eventually hear what we need to, and usually nothing
more. That process is always enriched when we develop the
habit of recording the course of our dialogue with God and
with life, telling our own ongoing sacred story. This allows
us to remember and revisit earlier chapters in some depth,
which, in turn, can shed tremendous light on encounters
with God in the present. We are able to see more clearly
how God has been actively engaged in shaping and guiding
the previous steps in our journey, and we realize what our
hearts have learned. Then we can grasp with more certainty
the true nature of those inward challenges we face in the
present chapter of our spiritual story.

In narrative, conversation, timeline, or journal form, these
stories tell the slow but certain transformation of our lives.
That's why they hold such power. There are few greater gifts
we can give to a friend than to set aside time and simply say,

"Tell me your story." And nothing builds more trust within a circle of colleagues than to provide the time and expectation for sharing with one another the stories of our journeys in faith and life.

Organizations, like people, also have stories, and effective leaders learn how to tell them. When our denominational staff met on retreat to examine how we were responding to the dynamics of change, our facilitators led us through a fascinating exercise in creating an organizational timeline, such as I've described for an individual. A wall was covered with sheets of butcher paper joined together, making a long horizontal space with a single straight line at the top stretching across about thirty feet. We were asked, first of all, to write along the top those dates that marked the chronological development of the Reformed Church in America.

Our denomination began in 1628, shortly after the Dutch settled New Amsterdam, later to be called New York, so that's one reason why the paper had to be thirty feet long. Staff persons were invited to fill in this historical blank space, noting times such as when our first seminary was founded, when the denomination became officially independent of the mother church in the Netherlands, when religiously motivated waves of Dutch immigration came to various parts of North America, when overseas mission initiatives were begun, and when developments after World War II solidified the institutional infrastructure of the denomination.

Then we were asked to add the times of various events and the names of persons who had had a decisive impact on the direction and mission of the Reformed Church in America. The stories of some key figures in the seventeenth, eighteenth, and nineteenth centuries were remembered, as well as a painful division in the nineteenth century that established the Christian Reformed Church. Many more events and people were cited in the last three decades, such as the formation of our racial/ethnic councils, the ordination of women, dramatic reorganizations, the impact of particular general secretaries, and certain defining events, such as the Mission 2000 convocation held in New York City.

As we stepped back, we began to look at our story and talk together until some common themes began to emerge. We saw how the sheer pace of change had escalated so dramatically for us as the twentieth century came to a close, which helped us all realize how we were living in a very different environment as a denomination than we had in the past. Further, we could see that our present context, requiring continual change and adaptation, was itself likely to continue for the foreseeable future. This timeline exercise at the retreat helped us to tell our organization's story so we could see how we were connected to our past, better understand our present, and embrace our journey toward the future.

These exercises to help an organization tell its story can be used with non-profit groups, congregations, educational institutions, and corporations. All have stories that need to be discovered and interpreted. It's a responsibility of a leader to see that happen in the life of an organization. We've noted earlier that successful leaders have an ability to see the "big picture," and a creative sense for knowing how various parts of an organization should relate to the whole; they have the capacity to hold a complex variety of factors together at any given time. But transformational leaders also see the long picture. They have enough detachment from an obsession with the present to help an organization understand its story, stretching from the past into the future so as to enable staff, members, or a constituency to see their specific contribution in the context of this longer narrative and feel greater meaning and value in their role as they place themselves within this story-line.

Some years ago, a notable pastor and friend, Harold Korver, said to me, "You've got to move through tradition into mission," a remark that has stayed with me because tradition carries key parts of an organization's story. Many leaders who see themselves as "change agents" assume that their most formidable obstacle is tradition, and beyond any doubt, change is often thwarted by power of "traditions" within an organizational culture. Yet tradition in and of itself is often not the real problem. Rather, those resistant to change for a whole variety of other reasons use parts of a tradition defensively to defeat change. Tradition, however, carries deeply held values embedded within the life of an organization. Some of those values may, in fact, need to be reexamined in achieving an organization's most desirable future. Other values need to be sustained and strengthened, but require a fresh means for their expression.

Thus, good leaders will learn how to "mine" an organization's tradition for the most effective nuggets that can sustain its journey to the future. Historically, most movements of reform, even when radical, go back to an institution's founding leaders and their ideals. The renewal of monastic orders came through a return to apostolic models of community according to the intentions of St. Benedict. The abolition of slavery and women's suffrage came through an appeal to the original ideals of the Constitution and Declaration of Independence. Martin Luther never intended to found another church but rather desired reform based on a return to biblical and theological principles he argued were at the foundation of Christian faith. Similarly, the Red Cross keeps alive the legacy of Clara Barton. The Methodist Church keeps looking anew to the insights and writings of John Wesley. We keep moving through tradition into mission.

Leaders don't always have to master all the details of the organizations they serve. But they do need to master the art of telling the organization's story, interpreting its present reality, and connecting its legacy to a promising future.

24

Leading from the Inside Out

At the opening of the South African parliament in Cape Town in 1999 during the last year of his presidency, Nelson Mandela called for a "reconstruction and development program of the soul." He had made clear that "our first task as government is to change and improve the basic living conditions of people" and had worked tirelessly to that end. "We are, however, learning every day that there is an even more basic task of reconstruction before us. . . . The best attempts by a government or authority will be fruitless if the people of a country do not experience a change within themselves," Mandela concluded.

Mandela's incredible power as a transformational leader came in part through the demonstration of change within himself. Prepared for the presidency by thirty years in prison and a lifetime of resistance against oppression and injustice, he acquired a stalwart, inspiring moral and spiritual courage that enabled him to rise above the hatred and recrimination that was so deeply embedded in the apartheid system of his country. He led from this inner strength and offered to all the people a vision of moral reconstruction to guide South Africa's future.

Another model of transformational leadership, Vaclav Havel, also went from prison to the presidency of his country. In a powerful address to the U.S. Congress in 1999, he said this: "Consciousness precedes being, and not the other way around, as the Marxists claim. For this reason, the salvation of this human world lies nowhere else than in the human heart, in the human power to reflect, in human meekness and in human responsibility. Without a global revolution in the sphere of human consciousness, nothing will change for the better in the sphere of our being as humans, and the catastrophe toward which this world is headed — be it ecological, social, demographic or a general breakdown of civilization — will be unavoidable."

Like Mandela, Havel knew how imperative was the task of building social, economic, and political systems that promote justice, freedom, and human dignity, but throughout his experience of repression in Czechoslovakia his conviction that fundamental change must find its roots in the wellspring of spirituality was sharpened and reinforced.

Mandela and Havel reveal something of the spirituality of leadership. That phrase can be easily misunderstood, but I contend that authentic spirituality puts us in touch with life's deepest realities and the truth about ourselves. Because they have encountered spiritual truths in the midst of deep and painful human realities, leaders like Mandela and Havel have helped whole societies embrace a new future.

The search for God is a quest to find life in its fullest and deepest expression. Opening our lives to God's presence places us in touch with Love that is at the heart of the universe. A life shaped by this divine encounter becomes intimately connected with the world's pain and hope, for these are carried in the heart of the Creator.

Leaders are often "outer-directed" personalities, artfully gauging people's daily reactions to them and scanning the faces in every room they enter to solidify old relationships and build new ones. But in today's world, I believe transformational leaders must also be "inner-directed," nurturing a disciplined journey into their souls, discovering how their lives can be rooted and grounded in God's love. Leaders cannot lead organizations beyond present, confining realities into a new and revitalized future unless their own lives have been opened to new possibilities wrought by the Spirit.

Normally it need not take thirty years in prison to become an inner-directed, transformational leader. But it does require liberation from the imprisonment of external expectations, demands, and preoccupations, and prayer is a trustworthy pathway leading to such freedom. At its best, prayer detaches us from the superficial in order to attach us to what is most real.

We can learn a great deal from those who spend much of their lives in prayer, for example, Father Thomas Keating, a Trappist monk living at St. Benedict's Monastery in Snowmass, Colorado. Keating is the author of the best-seller *Open Mind, Open Heart,* as well as several other books on prayer and life. He founded Contemplative Outreach, described in its vision statement as "a spiritual network of individuals and small faith communities committed to living the contemplative dimension of the Gospel in everyday life through the practice of Centering Prayer." This network has grown into 140 informal chapters around the world with a continuous program of prayer retreats and workshops, a sign of how hungry people are to center their lives in God's presence.

Keating stresses how prayer frees us from false illusions about our self as we encounter the life of the Trinity. Such an encounter connects us to the deepest realities in the world. In his words, "Contemplative prayer is not a narcissistic or self-preoccupied adventure. As it develops, it increases our concern for the needs and rights of others as well as our sensitivity to our belonging to the universe and to the whole of creation. . . . Our prayer is healing us of the self-centeredness and the thought that we are the center of the universe." Everyone who has the responsibility of leading others needs to draw from such wisdom.

Three decades ago, as a young aide on Capitol Hill, I was exhausted from the 1972 political campaign and thought I wanted a vacation in the Caribbean. But on my desk was a note with the phone number of the guesthouse at a monastery. I had never set foot in such a place, but I dialed that number instead of my travel agent. And so by chance, or rather providence, I nervously made my way there. It was a revelatory week for me and, as I shared earlier, changed the course of my life. Old words I wrote then in my journal now yellowing still sound fresh today. "Love is at the heart of the universe for Christ is there. Love propels and drives all life; it pushes its way up through the cracks and crevices, between the rocks and stones of hatred and suffering. There is a force behind it all; love is at the heart of it all, for God is there. . . . Of course, in every person, and in the corporate life of humanity, the powers of evil can be strong and grim. . . . But at every point, in every life, in every group, in every nation, at any point, the love of Christ, the source and root of the universe, can break through and flow, making all things new. My call is to be in the flow of that love."

We all need to keep discovering and returning to those places and practices that allow such love to break in, so we can lead from the inside out.

25

The Model

We can discern a pattern in the interaction between a leader and a community as it moves through its cycles of formation, growth, and transformation. Organizations move from vision and mission to strategy, goals, plans, and a changed future. Leaders change in their style accordingly, or else they inhibit growth. Organizations have journeys of hope, frustration, and promise like wagon trains crossing new frontiers. Even small teams mirror these same cycles as they form, storm, norm, and perform. In time frames of months or of decades, institutions move through stages of birth, cohesion, growth, conflict, and renewal or decay, with leaders always playing decisive, but evolving roles.

Are these patterns somehow intrinsic? Is there a model for leadership that transcends history and cultures, and has a revelatory significance? I believe there is such a model found in Jesus Christ.

Beyond doubt, historians from any religious or cultural background will acknowledge that Jesus of Nazareth was one of the most influential leaders in the entire history of the world, for this leader and those who followed in his way fundamentally altered the course of world history. Two thousand years after his death, the world's largest religious faith bears his name.

Christians, of course, believe that Jesus was more than a model; he was the uniquely incarnated presence of God in the life of the world, and his life, death and resurrection are the means of salvation and wholeness for each person and the entire world. Nonetheless, Christian or non-Christian, one can ask a simple and fair question: How did Jesus lead? Did he show us a style or pattern of leadership? Did he demonstrate timeless truths about all leaders and their communities, truths that might still guide us today, even in the massive organizational complexity of our twenty-first century?

Jesus began his brief three-year-long ministry by proclaiming and casting a powerful vision, taken from the prophet Isaiah, and recorded most clearly in Luke 4:18–19. "The Spirit of the Lord is upon me, because he has anointed me to bring good news to the poor. He has sent me to proclaim release to the captives and recovery of sight to the blind, to let the oppressed go free, to proclaim the year of the Lord's favor." The vision, developed in Jewish tradition, became crystallized through Jesus into a fresh and startling mission. Luke notes that Jesus, at the start, "was praised by everyone."

After announcing his vision and mission, Jesus began inviting and calling followers, beginning with fishermen who left their nets, and including a tax collector, a Zealot, or political activist, and others in a widely diverse group united by a common call and mission. From the start he began nurturing them as a core community of those who would live out the vision he was proclaiming, inviting those who had questions to "Come and see" (John 1:39). He was unambiguous in his call for commitment, asking for decisive fidelity to the mission, but he took all the time necessary to shape this diverse group into a community committed to one another.

His vision was elaborated and was continually reinforced through imaginative examples and penetrating stories concerning the kingdom of God. He described its life as a sower sowing seeds, as yeast in a loaf, as a mustard seed, as a lamp taken out from under a bushel, as treasure hidden in a field, as a merchant searching for pearls, as a net thrown into the sea, as new wine in old wineskins, and in many other ways. People were being offered hope and promise for a new way of living together. Further, Jesus kept clarifying for his followers, on famous occasions such as the Sermon on the Mount, the radical values and changes in behavior that would lead to this promised future. Moving phrases and penetrating stories described those different ways of living, acting, and relating that were expected for the implementation of this vision.

Next, as his community began to internalize this vision as their own, he further empowered them to carry it out. First, he sent his twelve disciples — what we might call his "core team" — out in groups of two to carry out the mission, proclaiming this coming kingdom, calling for the change of hearts, and healing those who were sick or tormented. Later, he sent out seventy followers in the same fashion, telling them to cure the sick and proclaim, "The kingdom of God has come near to you." So Jesus announced the vision and worked to plant it in the hearts of his followers, enabling them to own the authority and power necessary to make this vision a reality.

Finally, at the end of these three years, when his mission was at its most decisive point, he placed all his trust, confidence, and hope in the hands of his closest followers. The

Gospel of John, in the thirteenth chapter, records how on the evening before his arrest and death, in the upper room with his disciples, he took a basin and towel and washed their feet, an act done only by lowly servants of a Jewish household in that time. Jesus was demonstrating what it meant to be a servant leader.

"Do you understand," he asked them. He was their Teacher and Lord. But now his sole intent was to serve them, and to show them how they were to relate to one another. He desired them to be fully empowered so they would live forth the vision he had initially proclaimed.

So Jesus began his ministry by announcing a radical vision and ended it by washing his disciples' feet. This reflected a movement of proclaiming a vision, focusing a mission, clarifying values, building a community, creating a new culture, and empowering a people to live out a transformed life together.

Theological perspectives, of course, can add far more to these truths. Christian faith proclaims that the resurrection of Jesus from the dead brought his living presence to his followers, and then the gift of the Holy Spirit empowered this community to be the body of Christ in the world.

But these first followers of Jesus came to embody the vision he had originally proclaimed. They then learned how to cast that vision to others and invite followers. They remembered how to nurture and train those new followers, empowering them to make this vision their own and carry it out. And they recalled how they were to lay down their lives for one another, even as Jesus had washed their feet. So the cycle continued.

That is how the church was born and continued to grow for the next two thousand years.

Of course, this history is also full of conflict, injustice, and terrible sin. We know all too well that the church remains vulnerable to human frailties.

Yet the pattern of Jesus and his community is a revelatory model. It shows us how leaders can function, how vision is incarnated, and how followers are empowered to become leaders.

Leaders and organizations in the twenty-first century face complexities that seem overwhelming, and a pace of change that feels uncontrollable. But there is timeless wisdom for us all to discover from a poor son of a carpenter, living two millennia ago in Roman-occupied Palestine, whose leadership and whose followers continue to change the world today.

Bibliography

Bandy, Thomas G. *Fragile Hope: Your Church in 2020.* Nashville: Abingdon Press, 2002.

Barger, Nancy J., and Linda K. Kirby. *The Challenge of Change in Organizations: Helping Employees Thrive in a New Frontier.* Palo Alto, Calif.: Davies-Black, 1995.

———. *MBTI Type and Change: Participant's Guide.* Palo Alto, Calif.: Consulting Psychologists Press, 1997.

Bennis, Warren. *Why Leaders Can't Lead: The Unconscious Conspiracy Continues.* San Francisco: Jossey-Bass, 1989.

Bennis, Warren, and Burt Nanus. *Leaders: The Strategies for Taking Charge.* New York: Harper & Row, 1985.

Bolman, Lee G., and Terrence E. Deal. *Leading with Soul: An Uncommon Journey of Spirit.* San Francisco: Jossey-Bass, 1995.

Borgdorff, Peter. "Tranformational Leadership in the Church." D.Min. diss., Western Theological Seminary, 1990.

Burns, James MacGregor. *Leadership.* New York: Harper & Row, 1978.

Clifton, Donald O., and Paula Nelson. *Soar with Your Strengths.* New York: Delacorte Press, 1992.

Cosby, Gordon N. *By Grace Transformed: Christianity for a New Millennium.* New York: Crossroad Publishing Company, 1999.

De Pree, Max. *Leadership Is an Art.* East Lansing: Michigan State University Press, 1987.

———. *Leadership Jazz.* New York: Doubleday, 1992.

———. *Leading without Power: Finding Hope in Serving Community.* San Francisco: Jossey-Bass, 1997.

Easum, Bill. *Leadership on the Other Side: No Rules, Just Clues.* Nashville: Abingdon Press, 2000.

Foster, Richard J. *Money, Sex and Power: The Challenge of the Disciplined Life.* San Francisco: Harper & Row, 1985.

Friedman, Edwin H. *A Failure of Nerve: Leadership in the Age of the Quick Fix.* Bethesda, Md.: Edwin Friedman Estate/Trust, 1999.

———. *Generation to Generation: Family Process in Church and Synagogue.* New York: Guilford Press, 1985.

———. *Reinventing Leadership: Change in an Age of Anxiety/Discussion Guide.* New York: Guilford Press, 1996.

Galbraith, Craig S., and Oliver Galbraith. *The Benedictine Rule of Leadership.* Avon, Mass.: Adams Media, 2004.

Greenleaf, Robert K. *The Servant as Leader.* Cambridge, Mass.: Center for Applied Studies, 1970.

———. *Servant Leadership: A Journey into the Nature of Legitimate Power and Greatness.* New York: Paulist Press, 1977.

Hall, Brian P. *The Genesis Effect: Personal and Organizational Transformations.* New York: Paulist Press, 1986.

Heifetz, Ronald A., and Marty Linsky. *Leadership on the Line: Staying Alive through the Dangers of Leading.* Boston: Harvard Business School Press, 2002.

Hickman, Craig R. *Mind of a Manager, Soul of a Leader.* New York: John Wiley & Sons, 1990.

Jaworski, Joseph. *Synchronicity: The Inner Path of Leadership.* San Francisco: Berrett-Koehler, 1996.

Katzenbach, Jon R. *Teams at the Top: Unleashing the Potential of Both Teams and Individual Leaders.* Boston: Harvard Business School Press, 1998.

Keating, Thomas. *Open Mind, Open Heart: The Contemplative Dimension of the Gospel.* New York: Continuum International Publishing Group, 1986.

Kotter, John P. *Leading Change.* Boston: Harvard Business School Press, 1996.

Malphrus, Aubrey. *Values-Driven Leadership: Discovering and Developing Your Core Values for Ministry.* Grand Rapids: Baker Books, 1996.

Morris, Danny E., and Charles M. Olsen. *Discerning God's Will Together: A Spiritual Practice for the Church.* Nashville: Upper Room Books, 1997.

Nouwen, Henri J. M. *In the Name of Jesus: Reflections on Christian Leadership.* Crossroad Publishing Company, 1996.

———. *The Return of the Prodigal Son: A Story of Homecoming.* New York: Doubleday, 1992.

Oakley, Ed, and Doug Krug. *Enlightened Leadership: Getting to the Heart of Change.* New York: Simon & Schuster, 1991.

O'Connor, Elizabeth. *Call to Commitment.* New York: Harper & Row, 1963.

————. *Eighth Day of Creation: Gifts and Creativity.* Waco: Word Books, 1971.

————. *Journey Inward, Journey Outward.* New York: Harper & Row, 1968.

————. *Letters to Scattered Pilgrims.* San Francisco: Harper & Row, 1979.

————. *Servant Leaders, Servant Structures.* Washington, D.C.: Servant Leadership School, 1991.

Olsen, Charles M. *Transforming Church Boards into Communities of Spiritual Leaders.* Washington, D.C.: Alban Institute, 1995.

Olsen, Charles M., and Ellen Morseth. *Selecting Church Leaders: A Practice in Spiritual Discernment.* Nashville: Upper Room Books, 2002.

Pascale, Richard, M. Millemann, and L. Gioja. "Changing the Way We Change." *Harvard Business Review* (November–December 1997): 126–39.

Quinn, Robert E. *Deep Change: Discovering the Leader Within.* San Francisco: Jossey-Bass, 1996.

Rice, Howard L. *Reformed Spirituality: An Introduction for Believers.* Louisville: Westminster/John Knox Press, 1991.

Ruden, Sarah. "What Happened to Allan Boesak?" *Christian Century* 117, no. 19 (June 2000): 670–71.

Tushman, Michael L., and Charles A. O'Reilly III. *Winning through Innovation: A Practical Guide to Leading Organizational Change and Renewal.* Boston: Harvard Business School Press, 1997.

Acknowledgments

Ideas are rarely original. They are refined through networks of dialogue that continually measure abstraction against experience. Many have shared with me the generosity of their reflections as we have sought to discern the relationship between leadership, spirituality, and organizational change. I mention only a few, whose friendship and insight have influenced the words on these pages: Dick Hamm, former President and General Minister of the Disciples of Christ (Christian Church), and a brilliant student as well as a teacher of religious leadership; Cliff Kirkpatrick, Stated Clerk of the Presbyterian Church (USA), who serves so graciously in one of the most arduous positions of denominational leadership; Father Ivan Marsh, who served for several years as an insightful spiritual director, and also read an early draft; Jon Lax, a valued friend, who shared his perceptive reactions to my first draft; Peter Borgdorff, Executive Director of the Christian Reformed Church, whose friendship as well as his dissertation on the subject of leadership have been so enriching; Gordon Cosby, founding pastor of Church of the Saviour, who has been both a model and mentor; Senator Mark O. Hatfield, from who I learned so much about leadership, courage, and faith; and Jim Wallis, a faithful friend for three decades who helped convince me that I needed to put these thoughts into writing.

Several others made this book possible. The Reformed Church in America, the denomination I love and have served for the past decade, which provided a three-month sabbatical for writing; the Louisville Institute, which provided a sabbatical grant to support this project; Doug and Diane Fromm, treasured friends, who offered their cottage on Cape Cod for isolated days of writing; my staff colleagues in the Reformed Church in America, who serve as a trusted community of mutual support, especially those I work with most closely — Ken Bradsell, Shari Brink, Susan Converse, Gregg Mast, Dick Welscott, Bruce Menning, Larryl Humme, Jeff Japinga, and Gloria McCanna; Jeanette Salguero, my administrative assistant, who is a constant source of support and inspiration, and who handled many logistical details with efficient grace; and Roy M. Carlisle, my editor at The Crossroad Publishing Company, who first challenged me to write out of my experience and has been a trustworthy editorial guide.

Finally, my wife, Karin, who shares with such love her heart and soul, has made possible a life's journey together that has welcomed the vocational and spiritual experiences reflected in these pages.

About the Author

The Rev. Wesley Granberg-Michaelson was installed as general secretary of the Reformed Church in America in 1994. From 1988 to 1994 Wes served on the staff of the World Council of Churches (WCC) in Geneva, Switzerland, as the director of the Church and Society division.

In the late 1960s and early 1970s Wes served for eight years on the staff of U.S. Senator Mark O. Hatfield of Oregon. During that time, he was a member of Church of the Saviour in Washington, D.C., which molded much of his understanding of how commitment, spiritual growth, small groups, and social witness shape the life of the local congregation.

From 1976 to 1980 he served as managing editor for *Sojourners* magazine. Subsequently he moved to Montana to establish and serve as president of the New Creation Institute, working on issues of Christian responsibility for the environment as well as the church's role in healing and health.

Wes graduated from Hope College in 1967, and from Western Theological Seminary in Holland, Michigan, in 1984.

During his service as general secretary for the Reformed Church in America over the past decade, he has continued his ecumenical commitments through chairing the Steering Committee of Christian Churches Together in the USA, being a member of the Central Committee of the World Council of Churches, and serving as Chair of the Board for Call to Renewal.

Wes is the author of four books and numerous magazine articles, which have appeared in publications such as *Perspectives, Sojourners, Christianity Today, The Christian Century,* and *Ecumenical Review.*

Karin and Wes live in Michigan and have two children, Jonkrister and Karis. Karin is the author of two books, *In the Land of the Living* and *Healing Community.*

Classic books on leadership from Crossroad

Joy Carroll Wallis
THE WOMAN BEHIND THE COLLAR
The Pioneering Journey of an Episcopal Priest

Foreword by Dr. Rowan Williams,
Archbishop of Canterbury

Joy's story, from wild youth, to unexpected calling to the ministry and prominent involvement in the struggle for the ordination of women, as well as a "tabloid"" wedding to noted American author, activist, speaker, and professor Jim Wallis make it unsurprising that Joy Carroll was chosen as the inspiration for the acclaimed television series *The Vicar of Dibley*. This is an insightful and humorous chronicle of Joy's demanding life as a priest, wife, mother, and transplanted Brit.

978-0-8245-2265-0, paperback

Henri Nouwen
IN THE NAME OF JESUS
Reflections on Christian Leadership

Featuring new study guide!

Nouwen calls us back to a truly Christian model of leadership, where leaders remember to base their activities in a life of prayer and discernment. In countless retreats, workshops, and seminars, as well as in private reading and study, over 150,000 people have read and drawn inspiration from this little gem of Christian leadership. You will too.

978-0-8245-1259-0, paperback

crossroad

Classic books on leadership from Crossroad

Carmen Renee Berry
WHEN HELPING YOU IS HURTING ME
Escaping the Messiah Trap

Carmen Renee Berry, best known as the co-author of the million-selling *girlfriends*, first appeared on the national scene with the publishing phenomenon that started everyone talking about the Messiah Trap and how to overcome it. With her unsurpassed ability as a writer and teacher, Berry shows how we can help others only once we learn to love ourselves.

"Messiahs try to be helpful wherever they go. Wherever Messiahs can be found, you can be sure they will be busy taking care of other people. Do you find yourself trapped in a relationship where you do all the giving and the other person does all the taking?" If so, you have fallen into the Messiah Trap. This book is your ticket out.

978-0-8245-2108-0, paperback

Support your local bookstore or order directly from the publisher at
www.CrossroadPublishing.com

To request a catalog or inquire about quantity orders, please e-mail
sales@CrossroadPublishing.com

crossroad